The
Courage to Grow

Life Strategies to Become the
Best Version of You

Kendra Logan

The Courage to Grow – Life Strategies to Become the Best Version of You
Copyright © 2019 Kendra Logan
ISBN: 978-0-578-50772-9

All rights reserved. No part of this publication may be reproduced, stored in a retrieval systems, or transmitted in any form or by any means – electronic, mechanical, digital, photocopy, recording, or any others – except for brief quotations in printed reviews, without the prior permission of the publisher.

Printed in the United States of America
First Printing - 2019

Dedication

You never know how much something means to you until you completely lose it or come close to losing it. I never knew how much my own life truly meant to me until every aspect of it was upside down, and I found myself lying on the hallway floor of my house contemplating whether or not to keep it or depart from it. Struggling marriage, past due bills, broken-down vehicle, strained friendships, tension with family, isolation – I truly felt like I had indeed failed in life. That feeling - thinking that you are a complete and utter failure in life is one of the worst feelings, and I would not wish it on another soul. However, that feeling can also be the motivation you need to finally make some changes in your life.

This book is dedicated to anyone who has ever felt like a failure in life… those who have sat and tried to figure out where they went left instead of right… people just like me who didn't know how to recover and bounce back when all that they have known is no longer in existence. This book is for you. My prayer is that this book reminds you that in spite of what the world is throwing at you, amid any storm, during what seems to be the darkest time – you are not a failure at life, and you are needed to fulfill your life purpose. If you are willing to dust off the ashes from the fire you came through, you will emerge better than before and with a testimony to help others. Here's to you - let's refine ourselves and evolve into the people we are destined to be.

CONTENTS

Acknowledgments   1

Introduction   4

Section 1: The Fundamentals

    1. Love Yourself   15

    2. Choose Happiness   21

    3. Have an Attitude of Gratitude   27

    4. Be Kind: Every day to Everybody   33

    5. Seek & Find Inner Peace   39

Section 2: The Habits

    6. Take Back Your Thoughts   47

    7. Live – Authentically, Out Loud, & in Color   55

    8. Forgive – Everyone & Everything   59

    9. Be Your Own Cheerleader   65

    10. Just Stop Complaining   71

Section 3: The Fun Stuff

    11. Create a Life Mantra & Live By It   77

    12. Travel – See the World   81

    13. Try New Things   87

    14. Create a Bucket List   93

15. Play like a Child	99

Section 4: The Miscellaneous

16. Be a Helping Hand to Others	107
17. Engage in Continuous Learning	113
18. Have Intentional Friendships	119
19. Don't Take It Personal	123
20. You Can't (and Won't) Please Everybody	127

Section 5: The Val-"You"s

21. Mind Your Mind	133
22. Sweat, Smile, Repeat	137
23. Find Your Spiritual Strength	143
24. Manage Your Emotions	147
25. Embrace Your Growth	153

Section 6: The Daily Reminders

26. It's Ok to Say "No!"	159
27. Take a Moment for Yourself	165
28. Always Do Your Best	169
29. Giving is Living	175
30. Love Everybody, Everything, Every day	179
Final Thoughts	183

Acknowledgments

Writing this book hasn't been the easiest task, and I thank God for giving me the strength to see past my shortcomings and keep at it. When writing this book, I stopped and started and stopped again, more than a few times. This book would not have been completed without the motivation, support, and most importantly, LOVE from some extraordinary people.

- **TRE'**
  I never would have thought that a quick introduction and a few hours of conversation in a black Camaro would turn into a decade long bond. This bond is inimitable, unbreakable, and no words can adequately describe it – it's Gibberish ☺ that only we can translate. Thank you for being there over the years as I have grown into THIS woman, THIS mindset, and THIS strength. The '09 Bonnie & Clyde -- we will forever be.

- **MY BABY BOY, IV THE JEDI**
  You are truly my SONshine and every aspect of my life is heightened because of you. Your force has been strong since the moment you arrived, and I am in continuous awe of the things you can do to bring sheer joy to me. Your silliness and your smiles motivate me more than any other. I said it before you were born – that you were going to be legendary, and I still believe it. Keep using your force; you are destined for greatness!

- **THE DOC**
  Your love and wisdom are undeniably one of the most genuine things in my life, and without it, I am completely sure that I would be lost. Thank you for motivating me to be great. One day, I am going to be like you and get that "Dr." in front of my name too.

- **THE MATRIARCHS**
  - **P.A.TEEZA** – Look, Mama, your baby girl did it! Thank you for ALWAYS reminding me of the Queen I am and the woman I am destined to be. There would be no me… without you.

  - **TAMMIE GIRL** – Thank you for letting me go through every imaginable emotion on your phone and after every single vent session saying, "Well, it's going to make a good book one day." Your continuous planting of this seed helped get me here.

- **THE TREMBLIN (SLEEVE, MZ.PHAT BOOTY, DEEZE)**
  Y'all have been there since Day 1, literally. Your constant questioning of "How's the paper coming?" helped me to actually get the writing done and put this to paper. Now I just have to use your question for its true purpose – my dissertation. It's coming - Just hold on, we're going home.

- **THE FUNDAMENTAL FIVE (THE BESTIE, THE MILLY CREW, & THE TRIFECTA)**
  Together we are truly the "Sophisticated Six," but y'all are MY "Fundamental Five." A woman could not ask for a better squad. Thank you for answering my texts at 12 am or 12 pm, praying for me, crying with me, and enduring life's obstacles by my side.

- **MY NEW YORK SISTER**
  Your support and LOVE is always right on time. I don't know how you know exactly when I need to hear from you, but your timeliness is impeccable. Thank you for sending love, hugs, and motivation from hundreds of miles away.

Introduction

The week before I turned 30, I was hit with a flux of mixed emotions. I found myself spending countless hours just sitting and thinking about my life and everything I was dealing with. I was a new mother, having just had my son a little under 8 weeks prior, preparing to return to the workforce full-time, and it just seemed like a bad time to turn 30. I wasn't ready. Unlike turning 20, when I couldn't wait to get out of the teenage years to separate myself from high schoolers, adolescence, and be a step closer to the legal drinking age, turning 30 just came with so much more "serious" stuff. Nobody wants to be the person in their 30s that STILL doesn't have their life in order. In society, it seems more acceptable to make "BIG" mistakes in your 20s because you are still in college or living with parents or trying to figure out your career path, but your 30s are meant to be the years in which you excel and essentially take your life to the next level.

So here I was, turning 30, and asking myself questions like, "Am I happy? Did I accomplish enough in my 20s? Where am I according to my life plan? Was I ready for the next decade, the dirty 30s?" Being the analytical person that I am, I completed several activities to help myself prepare for this transition into 30. I made a list of all my accomplishments from my 20s, and while the list was fairly lengthy and I had indeed accomplished a great deal, I still felt like I needed more before 30. I looked at old pictures on my computer and social media of various events from my 20s. I laughed at my growth in fashion, style, makeup, and so many more areas. But even with that visible growth, I felt like something was still missing. I looked at pictures from some of the most important and best days in my life… graduating from college twice, my wedding, my business launch, my first

BBWIW event, my baby shower, my son's birth and thought about all the things I wanted for myself, my friends, and my family before 30. It was all surreal. Ten years, an entire decade, had passed, just like that and I honestly couldn't believe it. I looked at my son, so small and innocent, and wondered if he was proud of his mother at 30. My friends and I had talked about turning 30 for years, but as it quickly approached, I didn't feel that excitement we had discussed previously. I didn't have an elaborate party or event planned to usher me into the next decade. I didn't have what I saw so many other people on social media had for 30. I just wasn't ready to turn 30, but I knew it was coming and there wasn't anything I could do about it because time waits for no one.

After a few days of contemplating all aspects of my life and realizing that 30 was coming whether I was ready or not, I decided to take a different approach to it. I concluded that undeniably my 20s were coming to an end, but every closed door leaves an opportunity to open a new one. I was going to close that decade called the 20s and open a new decade. Closing the door to my 20s didn't mean that I was going to forget everything about it, but instead, I'd take all of the lessons that I learned from the past 10 years, put them in my custom Lady Logan duffle bag, and take them along with me into my 30s. I also decided one other thing - that I didn't want to "wing" my way through life anymore. I didn't want to find myself turning 40 and looking back at my 30s in the same manner that I had just looked back at my 20s. I no longer wanted to feel like I wasn't ready for the next decade, or next year, or even the next day for that matter. I wanted to move forward with the idea that every day that I had on this earth was going to be prosperous. I wanted to live in such a way that I would be excited to see what the next day would hold. I was ready to live THAT life - the life that so many people dream about, the flourishing life, the prosperous life, the successful life. Now don't take that to mean I thought I would not have my share of life's tribulations – because let's be real, there is no such thing as a perfect life, a perfect person or a perfect anything. However, this new mindset that I was ready to exemplify daily would not allow my struggles to defeat me or my mistakes to define me. My mind was ready, and I was set to do this… 30 with a new attitude and goals to work on me and create the life I desired. The only problem was - I wasn't sure how to create this life I wanted or how to achieve this new best version of me. How do I get there? So, first things first, I decided to embark on the journey of learning what steps I needed to take, what things I needed to do, what mindset I needed to grasp to become the best me and achieve my happier, successful life. I decided to give myself 365 days, the first year of my 30s, to learn everything I needed to know about personal growth and by my 31st birthday be living my own successful life. It was an interesting Year 30 with its own ups and downs. I have researched the greats, read books by some of the best, but most importantly, I have lived, and I can honestly say that I believe the saying that life is the best teacher. After everything, I have discovered 30 tactics to employ to gain that life that you want… to grow into the best you. Here I am sharing my knowledge with you and so glad that you want to take your life up a level and achieve your own prosperous life. I hope that you are ready to do what it takes to move your mindset into a place of positivity and peace, and in return, enjoy life as we are supposed to. Here's to your successful life! Enjoy….

The Courage to Grow:
Life Strategies to Become the Best Version of You

The Fundamentals

1

Love Yourself

•

Love yourself, flaws and all, because without your flaws, you wouldn't be you; and you were created for a unique purpose, no matter what anybody else says or thinks.

•

1: LOVE YOURSELF

The basis of life is LOVE, and all things for your life begin and end with you. Therefore, we begin with loving yourself. Loving yourself sets the tone of your life. Loving yourself first puts the action on you, and you are the only person that can change aspects of your life.

I know it sounds easy, and we hear it all the time. Accept yourself. Know your worth. Love yourself, even if no one else does. People will always say that statement as if implementing it is effortless, but in reality, it is not. In today's society, it is the norm for people to depict themselves in a way that may not be as realistic as they would hope, especially on the internet and social media. It's difficult to NOT compare yourself to what you see. I, myself, have been a victim of this more than a few times. There have been numerous times when I found myself wondering:

- Why is this happening to me?
- Am I not enough?
- Why didn't they like this or that?
- Why can't I be like her?

It was during these times, when the love for myself was at its lowest and I doubted my ability to be what I needed to be or do what I needed to do. This resulted in an unhappy life and an unhappy me. You must love yourself before you can love anyone else and in order to be the best version of you. It is impossible to be the best you if you hate yourself and everything about you. Strive to love yourself unconditionally. Here are some tips to help you along the way:

THE FUNDAMENTALS

1. **IMPROVE YOUR INNER THOUGHTS AND VOICE – ONLY POSITIVE THOUGHTS AND WORDS**
   Remove negative thoughts about yourself from your mind and negative words about yourself from your vocabulary. Yes, we have all things about ourselves that we can work on, but that does not equate to downing yourself in the interim. Speak truth and positivity about yourself, and the truth is that no matter where you are in life or what things you feel need to change about yourself, you are still beautiful and awesome. Love yourself with all your flaws.

2. **AVOID PERFECTIONISM, EMBRACE FLAWS – YOU ARE PERFECTLY MADE JUST THE WAY YOU ARE**
   There is no such thing as a perfect anything, especially a perfect person. Instead of doubting yourself because of your imperfections, embrace your flaws. I am short and petite, always have been and very likely always will be. It took me a long time to embrace it – especially with all of the short jokes that I have had to endure over the years. After I had my son, my body wasn't the same. While I love some of the changes, others made me want to wear a Spanx all day, every day. It wasn't until I decided to embrace my stretchy skin, scars, and pouches and love myself with all of the mommy flaws that I was a better me. Those things make me, Kendra the Mommy, and that role is one I wouldn't change for the world.

3. **DON'T COMPARE YOURSELF TO OTHERS**
   It may seem like celebrities are perfect, or people on social media have it all together, but at the end of the day, they are just the same as you and me - human. They eat, sleep, and think just like any other person. Love yourself for who you are, what you have done, and

where you are going, instead of comparing yourself to the limited snapshots you see online via social media of others. They may look perfect from the outside, but there is always more than what meets the eye. You never know what someone is going through behind closed doors and when the cameras are away.

4. **DAILY POSITIVE AFFIRMATIONS**
If you tell yourself something enough times, you will begin to believe and focus on it. This is how pathological liars are able to pass lie detector tests. Therefore, instead of affirming negativity on yourself, affirm positivity daily about how awesome you are. Tell yourself you are beautiful and perfectly made. Remind yourself of the marvelous things that you contribute to the world.

Starting right now, make a commitment to LOVE yourself and the purpose you were created for. Embrace the person you are and look forward with delight at the person you are becoming. Believe in yourself like no one else can and remember that YOU are special, you are enough, and no one should make you feel otherwise.

Below is the Love Yourself Promise. Say it every day to remind yourself of who you are and how awesome you are.

Love Yourself Promise

From this day forward, I promise that I will treat myself as someone uniquely special and as someone I deeply love. Through my daily mindset, thoughts, words, choices, and actions, I display my love for myself. I am an amazing soul and have a purpose exclusively for me.

2

Choose Happiness

•

The secret behind true happiness is the recognition and acceptance that you carry the ability to choose to be happy.

•

2: CHOOSE HAPPINESS

It has been scientifically proven that the happiest people in the world are those who recognize that they control their own happiness and that happiness is a choice; therefore, they choose to be happy. Every day that they are given on this earth, they actively practice choosing to be happy throughout the day and night and so should you! I know that choosing to be happy is a lot harder than it sounds. If it was truly that easy to just be happy, I'm sure that many more individuals across the globe would be happy. When things are not going as planned, or life decides to whack you in the face with a bag of bricks, it's hard to be happy. You just want to lie down, cry, and be sad.

Trust me, I have been there and done that more times that I want to admit. I have spent weeks of my life just lying in bed crying, wishing for things to be different, hoping for some positivity, asking the dreaded questions like Why Me? What did I do to deserve this? And what did I get from this? Fifteen pounds lighter (which is never good for a person of my size and stature) and a weakened immune system. The reality is that being sad or mad and lying and moping around is making you miss out on doing things that someone else is wishing they were able to do or losing precious time that someone else wishes they had.

Becoming the best version of you and achieving the life you desire require being able to choose happiness despite your circumstances, possessions or the people in your life. No one else should have the ability to control your happiness. It belongs to you. Don't get the wrong idea – I recognize that it is unrealistic to be happy ALL the time. Everyone is human, and we are built to have and experience various emotions: mad, sad,

THE FUNDAMENTALS

hurt, etc., and that is fine. It's acceptable and natural to experience those emotions but not for lengthy periods. Being sad for days is unhealthy. Being mad for weeks steals your joy. Being hurt for months stunts your progress. Learning to love your life despite the state that it is in is the key to happiness and happiness is key to your success and being the best version of you.

How do you start to choose happiness? Here are 4 actions to support choosing happiness – starting now:

1. **TAKE LIFE ONE MOMENT AT A TIME**
   When something happens that you didn't plan for, it's so easy to get caught in a whirlwind of emotions and thoughts. On top of that, you start to remember things about the past and worry about things in the future that haven't even occurred yet. All of those things are killing your growth and keeping you stagnant. Instead, focus on a single moment at a time. Whatever happened yesterday has already occurred and cannot be changed; therefore, dwelling on it will serve you no purpose. What will happen tomorrow is unknown, tomorrow isn't promised to anyone; so don't waste good energy focusing on the couldas. Instead, focus your energy and thoughts on what you can control, and that is this single moment and second. Right now is all that we have, so be happy in this very instance, and then the next… and the next.

2. **FIND THE GOOD IN EVERYTHING**
   I know that it may not seem like it, but I promise you that there is a little good in EVERYTHING that is happening to you. Whether it is teaching some lesson or saving you from something. All you have to do is find

that good. Your relationship is over, and you are heartbroken; well, that broken heart may be the motivation that you need to accomplish something. That relationship may have taught you what not to do in relationships, so when you get in the next one, it's a better relationship. That relationship being over will set you up for the person who you are truly supposed to be with. Choosing happiness includes finding the good and making it a reason to be happy.

3. **COUNT YOUR BLESSINGS**

    Happiness comes when you choose to reflect on the positive over the negative. Do you have breath in your body? You're blessed. Are you able to read this book and be of sound mental capability and judgment? You're blessed. There are so many things that can go wrong, but for every one thing that is going wrong, I can point out two things that are going right. Set your mind on your blessings and be grateful for the things you have. There is ALWAYS something to be grateful for.

4. **CARRY A SMILE IN YOUR BACK POCKET**

    A smile goes a long way, and you never know how it can impact not only your day but the day of others as well. Always keep a smile in your back pocket and whenever you feel yourself being sad or unhappy, pull it up, put it on, and brighten up your day. Is there a co-worker or close family member having a rough time? Time to take out that smile and spread a little cheeriness to the lives of others that you love so dearly; besides, you want them to be happy, right? The smile in your back pocket is a handy tool that has the power to make any day better. Smiles are made to bring you or someone else a little happiness - don't neglect to use it.

3

Have an Attitude of Gratitude

•

Life is never going to be all sunshine and roses, but when you have an attitude of gratitude, you realize that there is always something to be grateful for. Everything may not be perfect, but everything is enough.

•

3: HAVE AN ATTITUDE OF GRATITUDE

Having an attitude of gratitude is something that every single person should have and expel into the universe every single day despite what is happening in your life on that current day. Yes, I said it, EVERY SINGLE DAY! When a close family member dies? Yes. When you lose your job? Yes. When the bills are past due? Yes again. When a relationship fails? Still yes.

All of those things just listed are pretty negative or sad things, but the important thing is to be grateful regardless of what is going on or happening at the time. Having an attitude of gratitude does not mean that you won't experience other emotions based on what is happening. It's ok to feel frustrated that your bills are past due. It's acceptable to be sad by the loss of a family member. It means that even though you are in a tough financial spot or missing a mother that you are still grateful for the breath you are breathing and the heart beating in your chest.

I recognize that it's hard to be grateful when it seems like your world is falling apart… to have an attitude of gratitude when nothing seems to be going your way. You think to yourself, "What do I have to be grateful for?" A few years ago, I was in a place where my entire life seemed to be upside down; my marriage, my job, my relationship with family and friends, my finances… and I asked myself that same question – what did I have to be grateful for? My life was not going as planned. I felt like I was a complete failure and embarrassing people who associated themselves with me. I wasn't sure if my marriage was going to make it any longer. I didn't know if I was going to be able to pay all of my bills next month. I wasn't even on good terms with family and friends because I felt like everyone was judging me and criticizing my decisions even though they weren't walking in my shoes. All of that was going on, and I was thinking day in and day out – what do I want to be grateful for? Then an associate of mine died, and it wasn't a situation where he had been sick in the hospital and placed on hospice but a situation where he went to sleep one night and didn't wake up the next day. His roommate found him and called 911 where it was determined that he had died... just like that. I was heartbroken and sad for this person losing his life so abruptly but also because a mother and father had lost their child and their family would have a void that could never be filled. But here I was doubting what I had to be grateful for – even though I still had breath in my body – how selfish of me. I realized that I had more than a few reasons to have an attitude of gratitude. That was a wakeup call for me and made me see things differently. Yes, my light bill may be past due, but I still have the lights on. I may be having disagreements with family members, but those family members are still alive. From that day forward, I decided to always strive to have an attitude of gratitude. Now, every night when I say my prayers before closing my eyes, there are a few sentences that I say:

> "Thank you for my life and allowing me to make it through another day. Because I know there is someone who woke up this morning who isn't awake tonight... and just the same there is someone who is going to sleep tonight who will not wake up in the morning. If that would happen to be me, I thank you for the time that I was granted on this earth, for without you, none of that time would be possible."

There are many benefits to having an attitude of gratitude, but they all point to the same key concept that an attitude of gratitude changes your life for the better. And isn't that the ultimate goal – the best possible life, full of happiness, health, love, and success. Take a few minutes and create your personal Gratitude List. Pull it out when you need a reminder of everything you have. You will be amazed at the things that you truly have to be grateful for.

4

Be Kind: Every day to Everybody

•

Kindness is that ingredient that everyone needs to add to every single day of their lives. Kindness is the thing that can change the world.

•

4: BE KIND: EVERY DAY TO EVERYONE

This one may seem like a long stretch, but I promise you that it is so worth it. You are probably thinking that I am delusional, but I am not. I am kindness – well, I try to exemplify kindness in all of my activities daily. Kindness is a part of my life mantra… be kind and I try to live in such a way where people associate the characteristic of kindness to me when they think of me. Like hey, Kendra is Kindness – it spews out of everything she does.

In today's society, it's more commonly believed that you should live in such a way where an eye for an eye is the premise; be prideful, fight back, and seek revenge against those who have done you wrong. I spent most of my 20s living life with such a belief. And in some cases, it is ok to hold your own and stand your ground for your cause, but even that can be achieved without being mean and ruthless to others. The truth of the matter is that sometimes the best way to fight fire is not with fire but the opposite. Adding more gasoline to fire is only going to create a bigger flame. Sometimes instead of giving people what everyone else thinks they deserve, give them the opposite. It is in those times when you face all challenges and fight your battles with kindness that you are the true winner.

So you ask… if being kind makes you the true winner, why don't more people participate in it? Well, because it's easier to be mean, to be rude, to fight back and attempt to hurt someone in the same way that they have hurt you, and unfortunately, easy is the road that most people want to take. But you – you are different. Why? Well, for starters, you are reading this book to try and cultivate a better, happier, more successful you. Everybody isn't interested in living a better life – they are just

THE FUNDAMENTALS

fine slumming it and being jerks for the entirety of their natural life. Therefore, because you are different, because you want to take the road less traveled, you are already winning. Here are 4 reasons why being kind every day to everybody makes for a better life and you becoming the best version of you.

1. **EVERYONE IS FIGHTING THEIR OWN BATTLE AND HAS THEIR OWN DEMONS**

    I know when someone does something really mean or spiteful to you, you aren't caring about why they actually did it but are more focused on the fact of what they did. In most cases though, there is a reason behind everything. That doesn't mean you will agree with the reason, but just remember that there is one. It is impossible to know what someone is dealing with in their lives or going through that may have caused them to act in a way against you. But it isn't fair for you to make assumptions because those can be false. I am a walking testament of a person who has dealt with plenty of things without a lot of people knowing about any of it. I was still going to work, volunteering, posting pictures with smiles, and trying to be the best wife, mom, daughter, sister, and friend – even while on the inside I was crying a river daily. That didn't mean it was acceptable for me to lash out at others just because. It doesn't make it ok for me to seek to hurt someone purposely. This doesn't give the person a pass for doing whatever they did; it just reminds you that while you are hurting, they are probably hurting too. My mother, Tammie Girl, used to tell me all the time that "Hurt people hurt people" and a happy, successful person doesn't strive to keep that cycle going but instead seeks to break it. Always be mindful that every single person may be struggling with something in their own life and way; therefore, showing kindness is always the winning approach versus trying to apologize later because "I didn't know that was going on."

2. **KINDNESS IS ACTUALLY A STRENGTH, NOT A WEAKNESS**
   The easy response is to fight fire with fire or get even with someone for doing you wrong. It is much more challenging to speak positively about someone that lied about you, to not cheat on someone that cheated on you, or to hold your tongue and not gossip about someone who was gossiping about you. I get it - it is human nature to want to retaliate and make that person feel the hurt and pain that you are feeling or felt, but being able to look past that and still show kindness to them displays your TRUE strength - a strength that not many people have. It shows your heart, makes you honorable, and demonstrates that you have the qualities exemplified by people who are happy and successful. It's tough, and I completely understand. I have been cheated on in relationships. Girlfriends have backstabbed me. I have been hurt by people who I thought truly loved me, and in spite of all that, there isn't a person on this planet that I have dealt with that can't call me, and I wouldn't be kind or try to help. This doesn't mean that we are best friends or talk every day, but I am still able to show them kindness.

3. **THE WAY YOU ACT IS A REFLECTION OF YOURSELF**
   Every single thing that you say, do, or think is a reflection of yourself. I am an avid fan of the old ABC television show, Once Upon a Time, and they are always talking about how doing bad things darkens your heart. On a regular basis, they are pulling out of the character's

heart to see the darkness taking over as they do more evil or dark things. I know it is only a TV show, but if you could actually look at your heart and see it affected by the things you have done in your life, what would your heart look like? I actively participated in things in the past that I am not proud of today; I have lied, gossiped about people, gotten into fights, and tried to make others hurt. I did all of those things because I was broken on the inside and lived in such a way that showed I wanted to get even more than anything else. My reflection in the mirror was a very angry woman. I was angry at all of the people that didn't appreciate me, angry at the men who didn't love me the way I deserved, and angry at God for letting these things happen to me. My anger was radiating out of me through my actions. When you are kind to others, it reflects on who and what you are. It wasn't until I started displaying kindness through my day-to-day actions that more people saw kindness in me and wanted to see it in themselves. Strive to reflect things that represent love.

4. **It's the Right Thing to Do**
Doing good and being kind may not feel like the right thing to do, but it is. You may feel like you are allowing someone to get away with something or allowing what they did to go unnoticed and unchecked is them not learning their lesson; however, you are actually elevating yourself differently. It breaks my heart daily to see people becoming accustomed to the negative. It's sad that doing what's right gets looked over regularly with little to no glance. Despite how it may seem, remember, wrong will always be wrong, even if everyone is doing it, and right will always be right, even if no one is doing it.

5

Seek & Find Inner Peace

•

The calming sense of having inner peace is the sunshine to any storm. Embrace it. Enjoy it.

•

5: SEEK AND FIND INNER PEACE

The world is a very chaotic place, and technology has only made it easier to spread information about the things happening daily. I wish the alerts on my cell phone didn't go off as frequently as they do about bombings, shootings, natural disasters, racial injustices, and other things around the globe that add more confusion and unrest to the world that we live in. This is the world that I am trying to raise a young king in. When the outside world is full of turmoil, and you have to deal with your personal world on a daily basis, it is easy to understand how someone can get caught up in a state of frustration or in a place where everything seems difficult, and you are bothered consistently. It wouldn't be uncommon to feel agitated about things, but one of the best feelings in the world is when you have accepted what is and found inner peace.

Mastering inner peace is considered a success in life and to have it means to have a healthier, happier version of you. When you have inner peace, your mental, physical, and emotional sides have a sense a calmness, a feeling of tranquility, a place of serenity, and these things make you better equipped to enjoy life. Why? Because your small problems remain small. You don't allow trivial things to escalate into out of proportion calamities, and if something major does happen, having inner peace helps you to objectively handle such situations with ease, clarity, and sound judgment. A happier, healthier version of you resides with inner peace, but to acquire it takes effort and practice. Here are 4 ways to actively seek and find inner peace in life.

1. **PRACTICE ACCEPTANCE**
   No matter what you do or who you are, there are just some things YOU cannot change. It can be hard to

THE FUNDAMENTALS

accept that, especially if you are one of those people who always want to win or have a need to be right. Having inner peace means accepting things as they are, and for what they are. It means that you accept people for who they are and situations as they are. That doesn't mean that you allow yourself to be mistreated or stay in a crappy relationship because "that is how it is." Instead, remove yourself from the relationship and for your peace; you must accept that you cannot change them. For many years, I was mad at a lot of people because I felt they did not do things as I thought they should. Family members didn't call me like I thought a family should, a best friend that acted more like a stranger, and people not celebrating their birthdays like I wanted them to. These things were upsetting me daily until one day my father told me that I couldn't be mad at my family for being who they are. He said that some people have never been one to call every day or even every other day, so why was I allowing this to bother me so much, especially when calling just isn't their thing? I needed to accept them as they are and be at peace with it. When I started to accept things and people as they were, I immediately found more peace with things and situations in life. Acceptance allows you to understand what you can and cannot change.

2. **ONE THING AT A TIME**

    Trying to do too much can create chaos, and chaos is the enemy of peace. We take on multiple tasks more times than we may want to admit and feel as if we have to get everything done right now – guess what? You don't. Handling one thing at a time creates a type of simplicity that goes with peace and tranquility. When you attempt to focus on too many things simultaneously, most times it makes for less effectiveness of everything, resulting in dissatisfaction and a lack of peace. Giving your undivided attention to one thing results in you being able to give your best to it. When you can give your best, you are more at peace with the results because you know you gave your all.

3. **UNPLUG AND ESCAPE FOR A WHILE**
Social media, the internet, television, cell phones, and email can all contribute to removing your inner peace. Why? Because they all have the potential to be the bearers of bad news and show tragedy. If you are consistently exposing your mind to these things, having peace is unlikely. Instead, try something different. Leave your work… at work. Limit your internet and social media activity in the evenings and over the weekends. Take your newfound free time to give your undivided attention to family, friends, hobbies, or yourself (alone time). Being unplugged allows you to clear your mind from all of the opinions that everyone else is giving, and an uncluttered mind results in a clearer picture and clearer decisions.

4. **LET GO**
The present is the present, just as the past is the past. If something happened in the past, that is negative and has been weighing on you for some time, or it's still on your mind – accept it, then let it go. When you truly accept something and let it go, it no longer holds power in your mind and can no longer take away your peace. The benefit of letting it go is that you can now re-direct your focus to what you are doing in the present to create a better future. Stop harboring whatever is holding you back. Let go and let God handle all of it for you.

The Habits

6

Take Back Your Thoughts

•

A thought is such a powerful thing, for what you grow in your mind is what lives in your heart and comes out of your mouth, ultimately creating your life.

•

6: TAKE BACK YOUR THOUGHTS

There is a saying that goes, "A mind is a terrible thing to waste." That statement is very true because learning is a life necessity, but just as important as learning is having a positive mindset. The saying should be rewritten to say, "A negative mind is a terrible thing to have" because what you focus on is what you see. What we think about and focus on will manifest itself in our attitudes and actions. If only we truly realized how powerful our thoughts are, we would strive never to think another negative thought.

The mind is a wonderful thing, and the power of positive thinking can actually create the life that you want. Let's really think about it. If all you are thinking about is negativity, will you have a good day? If everything that comes out of your mouth includes couldn't, shouldn't, wouldn't, or didn't, will you ever accomplish the goals that you would like to? "Think positive thoughts, speak positive words" is another example of a statement that so many people say but don't actually take seriously. Why? Because they are just thoughts and words, and thoughts and words can't actually change a situation, can they? Well, yes and no. Thoughts and words can't actually change a situation, like an action, but they can change how you view a situation, which can change how you react towards a situation, which can change how someone reacts to you, which can change the actions that someone else takes, which can then change the situation. It's a chain reaction, so when you throw some positive thoughts and positive words in the direction of your life, the likelihood that you will receive positive changes to situations increases greatly. The thoughts that you think can determine your future and what will happen tomorrow; therefore, let today be the first day of a new positive thought process where you take full control of your thoughts and strive to put your focus on positive thoughts versus negative ones.

Don't worry - you are not alone in this battle. I have been through extended periods of negative thoughts. I went weeks and months with nothing but negative thoughts about the things that I was going through and dealing with: my marriage, my relationships with family and friends, my job, my finances, etc. People would ask me simple questions like, "How are you doing? How is work? How is life?" And my negative thoughts would immediately lead to a sarcastic comment, or even worse, a negative comment. For example: Question - "How's it going at work?" Answer – "I hate that place. I loathe going there daily. I cringe at the sheer thought of arriving there in the morning and count down the minutes to my departure as soon as I arrive." I remember that question and response so vividly because I will never be able to forget the face of the person who asked the question after they heard my response. They looked at me with such shock and ended the conversation very quickly with a simple, "Uhh ok, sorry to hear that." Looking back, why wouldn't they? Who wants to converse with someone who is only giving negative energy and vibes? For years, when I was unhappy with my life, negative thoughts flooded my mind day in and day out, and it never made me feel any better, only worse. Thinking and saying negative things all day didn't make friends want to hang out with me more, but the opposite. As I was turning 30, I thought and said a lot of negative things about my birthday and why I didn't want to turn 30 because of everything I had going on. Nonetheless, that didn't stop my birthday from coming. So, how do we put positive thinking into daily practice and change our lives for the better? Here are a few strategies to help you gain total control of your mind and take back your thoughts for the betterment of your life:

THE COURAGE TO GROW

1. **START AND END EACH DAY WITH A POSITIVE AFFIRMATION**

   The first thing and the last thing that you think about every day set the tone for your day and your night. Ever notice how when you go to bed in a bad, sour mood, your sleep is less restful, or you toss all night? What about when you wake up on the wrong side of the bed and start the day mad? In most cases, does the day get better or continue in a downward spiral? Start and end each day with positivity. Every single day when I wake up, the first thing I think and say is, "Thank you for allowing me to see another day…" not "here it goes, another day that I have to go to work. I hate getting up for work," and the same thing applies at night. Every night, as I get in the bed, I say, "Thank you for allowing me to make it through the day." Your positive affirmations don't have to be thank you for life but make sure that they are positive and put you in the best mindset and feelings to start and end your day.

   Examples:
   Morning Affirmation: Today is going to be a great day.
   Night Affirmation: I am going to have peaceful, satisfying sleep tonight.

2. **SURROUND YOURSELF WITH POSITIVE PEOPLE**

   Take a good look at your circle. Does it include a lot of people who are negative all the time? There is a saying that you become who you spend the most time with. If your closest family and friends are negative people, they are going to create additional negative space and negative thoughts in your life. Negativity is infectious, and once it's spread to you, it's hard to remove. Try to surround yourself with positive people who will speak life into your situations and bring happiness to your life. By doing this, you are more likely to be a more positive person. This is a prime example of how "Birds of a feather flock together." Make sure you are flocking with positive people.

3. **CONTROL YOUR SELF-TALK**

Self-talk can put you in either a good space or a bad space. If the majority of your self-talk is negative, then your feelings, your actions, and everything else will follow that conversation and ultimately result in a negative life and a negative you. Control your self-talk. Make sure the things you are saying to yourself are uplifting and positive. Remember all of the things that make you awesome, unique, and like no other person on this planet. Put all of that greatness into your self-talk. Speak positivity to yourself and positivity will display itself in all that you do.

4. **REJECT AND REPLACE NEGATIVE THOUGHTS**

As soon as you realize that you are having negative thoughts, you have the ability to reject them. Do it immediately. Stop the thoughts directly and refuse to give them any attention. Toss them aside quickly along with all of the feelings or emotions that were tied to those negative thoughts. As soon as you have rejected the negative thoughts, replace it with a positive, truer thought.

Example:
Negative Thought to Reject: I hate my job. I want to quit every day.
Replacement Thought: I am not in the best place at my job, but I am lucky to have a job. I will try to find

another avenue at my job that I may like better.

The average person has somewhere between 50000 – 70000 thoughts per day. This breaks down to 35 – 48 thoughts per minute. If the majority of those thoughts are negative, it is impossible to lead a life of joy and happiness. Make your thoughts positive, and create the outlook on life that you truly want and deserve.

7

Live – Authentically, Out Loud, & in Color

•

Show up, be fearless, and live your life exactly as you want. When you live authentically – there is no better life than your own.

•

7: LIVE – AUTHENTICALLY, OUT LOUD, & IN COLOR

It may be cliché, but the saying is true - life is short. It truly is, and it seems to get shorter the older that I get. I hear and see more deaths of young people than I ever did when I was growing up, and it's heartbreaking. The number of my high school classmates that have already passed is shocking; it's so shocking that a few years ago, the local TV station from my home town did a story on it. Every time, I get notified of the passing of someone that I know whether it was expected or not, it still hits home a little more. In recent years, two good friends of mine passed, and it was really "a slap in the face, snap out of it" type of moment for me. One friend was one of the kindest guys I ever knew. He was always supportive of my endeavors and consistently told me that I could accomplish anything I wanted to. He was always in my corner and reminded me I would do great things. The other friend was a great guy – a fellow Libra, so we instantaneously had a connection. He was at my wedding, part of the wedding party, and was one of the realest people I have known. I didn't always agree with him, but even when I wanted to be mad at him for something, I couldn't because he was always honest with me about whatever he was doing or why he was doing it.

These deaths took a toll on me because I didn't see them coming. If you know me, you know that normally I don't do much anymore. I don't go to a lot of places. After being pregnant and having my son, I basically disappeared into my house permanently. It's not because I didn't want to do things, but I was allowing my fears of judgment to keep me in my house. I didn't want to be questioned about my life. I didn't want the strange looks from people trying to decipher what's going on in my life. I didn't want the eyes of society judging my weight loss (or gain). I didn't want prying people to see my sadness as I attempted to juggle life and its problems, so I figured I would just stay behind my closed doors. There I can control the narrative and what is visible to the public eye. But like I said, when my friends passed, it was a shock to my heart. I couldn't hide in my corner anymore because I really wanted to go places and travel, take my son on trips, and do more things with my family and friends without caring what anyone said, asked, did, believed or posted. As long as I am not maliciously hurting people or seeking to ruin another's life, why should I care about the judgment of others or what they are saying about me? It's my life, and I deserve to live it to the fullest every single day.

The happiest people that are the best versions of themselves know how to live their lives authentically, out loud, and in color. They own what they are doing and do not care who sees or talks or posts about it. They live because they remember that life is precious and it's a gift to receive it every single day. Enjoy life... sleep on the good sheets and eat on the china that has been sitting in the china cabinet for 12 years waiting for "a special occasion." Try a new restaurant food, watch a movie in a foreign language, travel and see some exotic places, and if you want to post it... DO IT. If you want to share it with only close friends or family, that's fine too! But please, live without fear of having to keep up with the lovey posts, successful posts, money posts, or whatever posts someone is posting on social media in an attempt to please the next person or for likes, comments, or shares. Live life for you and enjoy everything that comes with it.

8

Forgive – Everyone & Everything

•

Forgiveness doesn't negate their actions. Forgiveness gives you freedom and removes their power to destroy your heart.

•

8: FORGIVE – EVERYONE & EVERYTHING

It's the F word... that's right - Forgive!! And this is critical to becoming the best you and having a happy, successful life. You must forgive everyone and everything. I get it. People have probably done some AWFUL things to you. Some of those things you may feel will warrant you to hold that black cloud over them and the situation until they die or you die, but you have to forgive them. Even if what they did was intentional, or if your life was never the same, or if they really don't deserve it. Forgiveness is essential.

For many years in my 20s, honestly, more like the majority of my 20s, I held on to the hurt and anger that I felt from various situations in my life - situations such as failed relationships, lost friendships, work discrimination, and more. The mere mention of someone or something would send me into a dark place, make my blood boil, and automatically ruin my day. Please don't let me happen to see something on social media regarding someone or a particular incident – instant anger. I would think to myself, "How dare they walk around living their life, looking happy when they did what they did to me!" It didn't seem to be fair or right. That was my mindset for a long time. Then, one day, I was put in a predicament where I had to interact with a specific individual who was on my "Trigger my Anger List." I remember the moment I realized that I was going to be in the same place, in a very close vicinity to them, and I got a pit in my stomach. I was feeling flustered, hot, and to make matters even worse, it was at a place and time where I was working. I really needed to be professional because this was work. This was money. It was critical that I figure out a way to deal with this NOW without ruining my makeup, affecting my attitude, or messing up business. As I was in the bathroom trying to pull myself together, I thought about it, and I asked myself why am I allowing this person to impact MY LIFE negatively? Obviously, she wasn't walking around on eggshells because of me – she was walking around like she was winning – smiling and cheery. Suddenly it hit me; something has got to change, and it starts right now with me forgiving her - even though she didn't even know that. I had to release myself from that pain, and I did. I was able to do what I needed to do in that situation with a smile on my face and "an enemy" 10 feet away. I didn't miss a beat. Was it easy? No. Was it worth it? More than these words can describe.

So you may be saying, "Well, you did that Kendra, but it isn't always that easy. What have you been through?" To that I say, "Yes, it is." Once you can completely grasp the concept of forgiveness and its importance, then it is that easy. I have been

- Cheated on in relationships
- Lied to
- Lied about
- Stolen from
- Betrayed by "best" friends
- Abused mentally, physically, and emotionally

Even after dealing with all of those things... after forgiving everyone and accepting apologies that I never actually received and probably never will, I can honestly say that there isn't a person that I hold any malice in my heart against. Now that doesn't mean that I am going to be best friends with them, but it does mean I can be in the same room with people that actively and purposely sought to destroy my marriage and speak. I can be in the same room with the guy who abused me. I can sit at a table with the guy who cheated on me. I can help a former best friend who betrayed me, and let me tell you, that feeling is the best feeling ever... one of the FREE-est feelings that exude sheer peace and happiness throughout your body.

It is beautiful to be free of that weight that not forgiving someone is holding on your mind, body, and soul. Everything is better when you are no longer bitter. Even more, it shows your strength when you truly forgive. Weak people hold and harbor, strong people forgive, let go, and keep pushing for the better. Forgive everyone and everything, and not because of them or for them, but for you. Because you love yourself and your life enough to do what it takes to be the best version of you - the forgiving version.

9

Be Your Own Cheerleader, not Your Own Enemy

•

Leave your past in the past, embrace your present, and imagine your brightest future.

•

9: BE YOUR OWN CHEERLEADER, NOT YOUR OWN ENEMY

You are made to do great things, and the person you are becoming is phenomenal! If someone else tells you that it's flattery, so why don't we tell ourselves these things more often? The saying, "You can be your own worst enemy" comes to mind, and that philosophy can hinder you from being the best you. Growing up, we are taught to have an idea of how we want our lives to be - spouse, the number of kids, type of house, kinds of cars, career, bank account amount, and a specific timeline attached to it. Then we work on a plan to get all of those things. I am an avid supporter of teaching people to plan their lives to the best of their ability, but I wish we added some additional knowledge about being flexible and adjusting our plan accordingly. Why? Because life happens (things beyond our control) and sometimes we just make poor choices – that's called growing up and being human. Everyone has a past and some things in their past they are probably not proud of. The problem occurs when you consistently beat yourself up over things that you have or haven't done by a certain time in your life. You don't have to be so hard on yourself. Instead of tearing yourself down, start to build yourself up. Pat yourself on the back for small accomplishments and the big milestones without a timeline attached to them. If no one is giving you praise, give it to yourself. Be your own cheerleader, not your enemy. Forgive yourself for your past mistakes, adjust your actions in the present, and create your brightest future. You are the master of your life – uplift it to where you want to be.

Need help to start cheering for yourself? Here are a few important things to remember:

THE HABITS

1. **NOBODY IS PERFECT, AND NO ONE SHOULD EXPECT YOU TO BE... NOT EVEN YOU**
   Perfection is overrated, and it's impossible to achieve. Nobody is perfect, no matter what they say or show to the world. Every single person has some flaws and has made some mistakes – that's part of being human and what makes you unique and who you are. No one should expect you to be perfect. You shouldn't even expect it of yourself. Instead, embrace your challenges and your mistakes, learn from your situations and missteps, and use that new knowledge to make better decisions going forward to create the future you desire.

2. **EVERYONE HAS A PAST**
   You may know someone who seems like they have it all together and their life is just flowing down a lazy river with zero issues. While that actually may be the case now, I can guarantee that it wasn't always that way. Everyone has a past. Everyone has and is going through something. Despite what you think, you are not the only one dealing with issues or done things they are not proud of. Sometimes I think about things that I have done in my life like fighting girls over nonsense, selling drugs, or altercations with boyfriends. I can admit that I was doing some crazy things, but those things only remind me of how far I have come and motivate me to where I am yet to go. Your past is yours, mine is mine, and just like a butt hole, everyone has one.

3. **HARPING ON PAST MISTAKES IS POINTLESS**
   The past is the past for a reason. It is behind you, and aside from it as a lesson, it serves no purpose to dwell on it and the emotions, attitudes, and people residing there. Instead of holding yourself hostage with negative

energy from your past, turn it into motivation to propel yourself into a brighter future. Let go of the weight from your past and focus on your better and brighter future.

4. **EVERYONE SHINES AT THEIR OWN TIME**
The sun and the moon have no reason to be compared to one another because they each shine at their appropriate and different times. Just the same, you should not compare yourself to any other person. Don't down yourself if you haven't accomplished something according to when society thinks you are supposed to. Whether you graduate from college at 22, 26, or 52, it is still a great accomplishment. Accomplishments do not have a pre-destined age or time assigned to them, but a person. Support yourself and achieve the goals that you are meant to in your own time.

Everybody makes mistakes; it's expected. You are human - it's inevitable. The same way you forgive others, do the same for yourself and leave your past in the past. If you lived and learned from your past, then you did what you were supposed to.

Be your own cheerleader – wake up and tell yourself, "A great person is now awake and today I will be magnificent. Today I will be a light to the world because I am awesome." No matter what you have done or what you are going through, you are awesome! If no one else tells you, tell yourself. If you do something great, reward yourself. Pat yourself on the back and applaud yourself for doing something great!

10

Just Stop Complaining

●

Life becomes a whole lot brighter when you trade a complaint for a compliment and whining for winning.

●

10: JUST STOP COMPLAINING

Take a moment and consider how much time you spend complaining on an average day. Now multiply that by 30 days in a month. Now multiply that by 12 months. Do you see that number? That is a lot of time that you are wasting complaining about things when you could be doing so much more. You could be doing something more useful, something more beneficial, or something less annoying. Yes, I said it. Complaining is annoying. Let's be honest, nobody really wants to spend time with someone that complains 24/7. They may put up with it because they love you, but they really don't want to. Think about it. If you are always complaining, always negative, always finding something wrong - that type of energy is a drain. People or things that drain others is a no go.

So the question becomes, why are you complaining about things in your life? What positive impact does complaining provide and to whom? If something is not providing positive feedback into your life, then why do it? The answer is because it's easy and it comes so naturally. It's what we have been a witness to our entire lives… people complaining.

What if you were given the news that you only had 24 hours to live? Would the things that you are complaining about really matter anymore? Will you waste additional time complaining about pointless stuff or will you begin to focus on the things that really matter and be grateful for what you do have at the current time?

I struggled with this issue just like everyone else. Normally, on a typical day, I would complain about work. I complained about being tired. I complained about all of the things I have to do and sometimes how I feel unappreciated for it. I complained about the traffic. I complained about slow drivers. I complained about food. I complained about people. I complained about a lot of things, but guess what? All of that complaining wasn't making me feel any better or helping me achieve any of my goals. It wasn't putting money in my bank account and wasn't creating any positivity in my life or the lives of others. It wasn't making the world a better place, and it was exhausting. Finally, I found myself asking why I was engaging in an activity that had absolutely zero value to me. I thought about it, and logically, that did not sound right. It's not enhancing my life or making me happier; therefore, it sounded like something that wasn't cultivating the life I was trying to achieve. The only answer was that it needed to go.

Complaining is taking you in the opposite direction of a person who is happy and living the life they want. It allows you to continuously focus on things that make you unhappy and situations that bring you down. Therefore, you must remove it from your mornings, noons, and nights. Embark on a No Complaining challenge for a day. Then after successfully completing a day, try a week, and then a month. In due time, a habit of not complaining will become a reality in your life. Ask your family and friends to engage in this challenge with you. You cannot realistically expect to stop complaining if everyone around you continues to complain. It's contagious. If you find yourself complaining or about to complain, switch it around - say something you appreciate, something that makes you smile or try to find a solution to the complaint. For example, I hate traffic, so I may try an alternate route or leave a little earlier. When your complaints are minimal or non-existent, being a happier and better person becomes a thing of the present and not just a dream.

The Fun Stuff

11

Create a Life Mantra & Live By It

•

When you have clarity of your purpose, you have clarity in your life.

•

11: CREATE A LIFE MANTRA & LIVE BY IT

What are some of the popular sayings about life? Some examples that I hear frequently are:
- Carpe Diem - Seize the Day
- Don't Worry, Be Happy
- YOLO – You Only Live Once
- Hindsight is 20/20
- Hakuna Matata!

While it seems fitting to say them from time to time as they pertain to what is happening in your life, these sayings are not YOUR life mantra. They don't represent you and your life purpose. Having a personal life mantra that is specific to you is extremely valuable to the process of becoming the best you and having a successful life. Plus, it's pretty cool to have a saying that you created that you can say is a representation of who you really are. So what is your personal life mantra and what does it do for you? Don't have a life mantra? Let's create one.

What is a life mantra? A life mantra is a short phrase that explains your purpose in life and helps you keep things in perspective. It serves several purposes in your life, such as:
- Providing direction, like a compass in a crazy world.
- Re-centering you when you drift off course and your life is in chaos.
- Returns you to your purpose when you feel disorganized and overwhelmed.
- Your true motivation and inspiration to be your best self.

How do you create your life mantra? Creating your life mantra may take a little bit of time. You must truthfully answer questions about yourself like: What makes you most proud? What does success mean to you? What do you want to be remembered for in your life? Spend time with yourself soul searching and determining what drives you to get up every single day and live. Look within and seek key components that you feel make life worth living. These are the things that you want to be in your life mantra. These are the things and words that represent you. When I turned 30 and decided to change my outlook on life, I started pondering the type of person I wanted to be, how I wanted people to think of me, and what I wanted to exemplify in daily interactions with others. I decided I wanted to also show kindness, generosity, and love to others daily, and that became my current life mantra.

My Life Mantra is **Be Kind. Be Generous. Be Loving.** These are the vibes that I strive to demonstrate every single day, and I make an effort to motivate others, thru my own actions, to display these attributes as well. To me, kindness, generosity, and love are missing in life more than ever, and only by bringing them back to the forefront can life on Earth begin to get better. I am Kendra G. Logan, forever serving kindness, generosity, and love. This is what I live by and live for.

As you grow over time, your mantra may change, and that's fine. Your life mantra is meant to represent wherever you currently are in your life. As you grow, learn, and become the best you, it may need altering, just like anything else. The key is to remember to make it personally reflective of you and no one else. Live life with a life mantra designed for you and exclusively used by you.

12

Travel – See the World

•

This world is so unique, so full of unimaginable beauty. Don't live a life limited to a single place or thought; go and see the world in all its glory and magnificence. Revel in its beauty and be at peace.

•

12: TRAVEL – SEE THE WORLD

There is an 11-year-old princess in my life who I admire like crazy. Her name is Shelly, and she is beautiful inside and out. Of course, she gets a lot of it from her mother, but I really admire Shelly. At the tender age of 11, she has traveled to and seen more unique places than I have in my 30+ years of life. Shelly is the daughter of one of my closest and dearest friends, and one thing that they do is travel. I can go on Snapchat and click on my friend's story on a random Tuesday, and they will be in Puerto Rico, Spain, Hollywood or Paris; I absolutely LOVE it! Every year around Shelly's birthday, I tease my homegirl and ask her, "What are you getting Shelly this year, an island?" And she always laughs! Shelly, at only 11, is already mastering something that will help her hone life skills and live the best life as she ages – the art of travel.

At some point in my life, I think around my mid-20s, I became a homebody. I traveled to California to be on Wheel of Fortune at 21. At 22, I went to Las Vegas. I rewarded myself with a cruise to the Bahamas for graduating with my Masters at 24, but after that, I become a homebody - a real-life homebody. I would go to work, church, and home, and I am not sure how I became that person. If I happened to bump into someone in the store, they would have to do a double take to make sure that it was actually me because I just wasn't out like I used to be. Since the cruise to the Bahamas in 2010, I can count on one hand the number of places I have been and the number of vacations that I have taken. Just the other day, my co-workers were taunting me about being "boring" because I told them that I hadn't left the Charleston, SC area in almost a year. After hearing my co-workers talk about their travels to Peru and week-long trips to Thailand or Spain, I realized I was truly missing out. All of these places looked so great in the pictures that I saw everyone post on social media. All of these places sounded great after talking to co-workers and friends, so why wasn't I indulging in the vast places that this great planet has to offer? I wasn't sure, but I knew that being a homebody didn't sound like an approach that I wanted to continue going further.

Please understand, there is absolutely nothing wrong with being a homebody, but I also want you to realize that there is so much world to see - beautiful, breathtaking places. Places that will make you cry, places that will make you admire nature, and places so astonishing that minuscule problems seem pointless. I will never forget how beautiful nature was and how minute my problems seemed when I was 500 vertical feet in the air parasailing with one of my best friends. Being the best you and living your best life includes traveling, seeing new places, and learning about other cultures. So many times we get caught up in the humdrum of day-to-day life (work, home, church, kids) and day-to-day problems (bills, sickness, schedules) that 5 years go by in the blink of an eye and we haven't left our city. I am a sad example of this, unfortunately. Traveling adds so much to your life and provides knowledge that can only be gained by being hands on. It's one thing to see Egyptian pyramids in movies and pictures; it's something completely different to see them in person. It helps build your self-confidence because it is likely that you will experience something unexpected on your trip that requires you to make decisions you never thought you would. It makes you cherish home more – being away from the familiarity makes you appreciate it. For example, after you sleep in a hotel bed for a week, all you can think about is sleeping in your bed and being back on your couch. Traveling teaches you new things. Being immersed in a different place allows you to learn new things like cooking, a language, customs and more.

THE COURAGE TO GROW

Having this new knowledge is elevating you by making your brain more active and teaching you which results in an updated version of you and more happiness in your life.

Last but not least, traveling gives you new experiences and moments to remember, and that is what life is about - collecting a magnitude of memories that tell the story of who you are and explain how you became that person. I haven't been to many places recently, but the few places that I have visited in my early 20s each taught me something that I can still use years later. Traveling helps develop you into a better person, so plan a trip. You can start by going someplace close, but eventually, venture out and see the world. Be safe, have fun, and enjoy the many things that this world has to offer.

13

Try New Things

•

Unexpected doors open in life when you leave your comfort zone and try something new.

•

13: TRY NEW THINGS

You may not realize it, but we spend the majority of our day doing the same tasks that we have done repeatedly for months and years, hundreds of times. Think about it – every day we wash our bodies, brush our teeth, get dressed, sleep, eat, go to work, drive the same routes, and so many more routine activities that have become second nature. This is our lives. Have you ever stopped to think about the activities that have become routine? The times you wake up, the time you eat lunch and dinner, the people you eat lunch and dinner with, the TV shows you watch, and the list continues. With these routines in place, it is understandable how you may not realize that we are cruising through life basically on activity autopilot. We are living in a vast world full of unique cultures, cuisine, terrain, and so much more – yet we have purposely limited ourselves to the "things we know." That doesn't mean that every day has to be different, but it does mean you should not be living every single day, month after month, year after year doing the same things.

As I mentioned above, I really do recognize how easy it is to do the same things year after year. I have done it myself, eating the same meals each week on the same day for months. Monday is Chicken and Rice, Tuesday is Tacos, Wednesday is Spaghetti, and so on. How mundane is that? While I am an advocate for having a schedule and proper time management to ensure that you are maximizing efforts in a single day, you can still spice up things by trying a new restaurant on a Thursday or planning an activity that you have never done before. Being your best self requires excitement, energy and learning about yourself by trying new things. It is time to make a binding agreement to yourself TODAY to start trying new things and participating in new experiences. Trying new things may just give you the boost that

THE FUN STUFF

is needed to jump-start your life in a new direction. There are so many benefits to trying new things, here are 4:

1. **LEARN MORE ABOUT YOURSELF - GET TO KNOW YOURSELF BETTER**

   I know that you are probably saying, "I already know myself. I have been me for many years, so I know everything I need to know about myself." That is true - you have been you for many years, but it is also true that you don't know everything about yourself because you haven't done everything. We think we know ourselves, and then we do something and realize that we have a distinct like or dislike for something that would have never been found if we hadn't tried something new. How do you know that you don't like sweet potato pie if you have never even tried it? You are more than likely living with an idea or taste of someone else's. Trying new things on your own will allow you a deeper understanding of yourself and who you want to become.

2. **OVERCOME FEAR**

   Often fear is the one thing that keeps you from trying new things. We are automatically programmed to think of the negative side. "What if I don't like it after this investment? What will the consequences be?" Fear is always present in just about everything that you do, but the same way that you overcome fear to participate in familiar activities, you can overcome fear to try new things. The mind always wants to make things seem worse than they are or will actually be. Trying new things stops fear dead in its tracks and opens you up to a new world of possibilities and experiences.

3. **BOREDOM REDUCTION**
   Do you remember how we talked about being in a rut routine with no spontaneity or anything new? Well, that is extremely boring, and life is not meant to be boring or lame. Life is all about living. Trying new things allows you to take a walk on your wild side and kicks boredom out of your mindset. Instead of sitting at home on a Friday night talking to friends about how bored you are, go out and try a new restaurant or find an activity that you've never done and do it. Watch a movie in a different language or different genre than you normally watch.

4. **GAIN A SENSE OF ACCOMPLISHMENT AND A CONFIDENCE BOOSTER**
   You know how good it feels when you accomplish something that you really wanted to do and that you put your mind too? You know how boss and unstoppable you feel when you get it done with no issues? Trying something new provides those same feelings with amplification because of the newness. You stepped out of your comfort zone and kicked butt on something new! It sounds awesome because it is awesome. Trying something new will result in you feeling like a total boss and that feeling – is one of the best in the world. Cheers to the BOSS life!

When you try new things, it says so much about your personal growth, and life is all about growth, going to the next level, and developing ourselves to be that person we were created to be. Don't miss out on your level up towards becoming the best you because of that pesky fear of deviating from the norm. For once, be a rebel and do something new. It may be uncomfortable now, but you will be thankful in the long run.

14

Create a Bucket List

•

Your life is yours, and you only get one, so do ALL of the things that you want to do.

•

14: CREATE A BUCKET LIST

Everybody gets the same 24 hours in every day, but what matters most is how you spend your 24 hours. I understand on most days, we are all living our lives which consist of the norms: work, home, family, school, church, sleep, etc., but what about the things that aren't "regular" everyday activities that you really want to do? Nobody knows when their last breath will be, and time passed cannot be regained. So, are you actively planning and making strides to do the things that you really want to? Yes, everyone has the same 24 hours, but time also waits for no one. What you don't want to do is wake up one day and have regrets about all of the things that you didn't do when you could because you didn't plan for it or you didn't care or because you were "busy."

There are many things that I want to do before my time on this earth ends, and to my dismay, I have done 3. I have been on national television, visited Las Vegas, and I have been on a cruise, but there is so much more I want to do. I want to go sky diving, see the Grand Canyon, visit Niagara Falls, go to Africa, ride an elephant, hike through a rain forest, shop on Rodeo Drive, scuba dive, swim with dolphins, and more. So why haven't I done these things? Honestly, I don't know. I can't use money as an excuse, or even time, because I spent most of my 20s with fewer bills and more time, and I still didn't do most of those things that I wanted to. As I age, I am learning the importance of doing all the things that you really want to in this life, so to live your best life and be the best you, you should create a bucket list and work to accomplish items on that list. Your bucket list doesn't have to be all elaborate crazy things - just whatever means the most to you - anything from keeping fresh flowers in your house every week, to learning to make a

THE FUN STUFF

delectable dish, to climbing Mt. Everest. All these things qualify to be on your bucket list. Create a list that embodies the life you want to live and the things that you want to experience. Then as you are marking them off as completed, you will recognize some of the benefits of having a bucket list:

1. **HELPS DEVELOP A MORE FULFILLING LIFE**
   Life should be fulfilling because you only get one. You don't need to waste it living as someone else would or for someone else, especially when the only person that you can truly live for and control is yourself. Your bucket list gives you something to strive for, activities and items to look forward to, and allows you to truly determine the kind of life that you want to live. By determining the things that YOU truly want to do within your lifetime, you are continuing to learn about yourself, expanding your knowledge, and creating the best version of you.

2. **A SENSE OF ACCOMPLISHMENT IS ITS OWN REWARD AND IS A FEELING THAT CANNOT BE DUPLICATED**
   What words would you use to describe your feelings when you finally accomplish something that you have worked hard to complete? That feeling is something unique within itself and normally creates a sense of pride and happiness within you. Satisfaction with yourself will grow as you achieve the items on your bucket list. Life is better as you see the items on your list being scratched off.

3. **WRITING THE LIST INCREASES THE LIKELIHOOD OF ACCOMPLISHMENT**
   It is a proven fact that writing down your goals significantly increases your chance of achieving them. It

takes something that was once in your mind and puts it on paper – no longer making it just an idea or a notion. Writing them down displays your commitment and motivates you to act on the goals.

4. **TEACHES TO VALUE TIME AND EXPERIENCE**
It's been stated before, and it can be stated again, time is precious, and once gone, it cannot be regained. It cannot be transferred or borrowed. Creating a bucket list assists you in valuing time and experiences because no one is promised another day, minute, or second. Live life now and live it to the fullest.

Create your bucket list, put it someplace where you can see regularly, and use it as a reminder of all the things that you want in life and as motivation to push yourself to achieve them. Life is all about growth, so "bucket-list it up" and start working to scratch things off, one by one.

15

Play like a Child – Have Fun Every Day

•

Unlock the closed door of play and allow your inner child to reveal them self.

•

15: PLAY LIKE A CHILD – HAVE FUN EVERY DAY

Watching a child develop during their first few years of life is an experience like no other. Being a witness to my own son growing over the past two years has taught me things that I didn't even imagine and opened my mind to new ideas. My son is a people person, and he loves to play and smile all the time. Even when I am trying to be serious or get him dressed or discipline him, he is still throwing the cutest smile at me and giggling and wanting to play. One day, I was telling my mother how all he does is laugh and play, and her response was, "That's great. That's how you want him to be. You don't want him to be scared or afraid – he's a kid; let him play and enjoy life." The last part of her statement, "let him play and enjoy life" stuck with me, and when he wanted to play with the boxes that toys came in versus the toys themselves, I let him. When he goes to the window and says, "Outside" in his little voice, outside we go and run in a circle until he falls unto the ground laughing and staring at the sky. It is truly a beautiful thing, and I began to wonder why we, as adults, no longer play like children and just laugh and run until we can't anymore. Clearly, we are born with an understanding of fun and experiencing life (kids are a prime example of this), but as we age and go into adulthood, somewhere along the line, we are conditioned to stop playing. "You are an adult now," they tell us, "time to grow up and worry about finances and jobs and bills and social media likes," but by doing so, we find ourselves unhappy and running a rat race. Becoming the best version of yourself requires opening yourself back up, finding your inner child, and allowing yourself to play and put fun back into every single day of your life!

How do you add fun back into your adult life? Here are a few tips:

THE FUN STUFF

1. **HIGH-FIVE**
   My son loves to high five and hands them out like candy. It doesn't matter what kind of mood he is in, if he hears the words "High-Five," that hand goes up, and he is ready to connect with you. Kids have no issues giving high fives, and the majority of the time they give them out for absolutely no reason, just because. Honestly, high fives bring cheer and happiness between the individuals. Add a little more fun to life by high fiving again. Got good news, give a high five and a boost of energy to another person or group of people.

2. **LIVE LIFE THROUGH THE CREATION OF THINGS**
   Kids are some of the most creative individuals on the planet. The way they create things with the most random objects and see things the way that nobody else does is phenomenal. Add a little fun to your life by creating; paint, draw, build, write, sculpt, plant, etc. Let your creative juices flow, and create something that is your own and free of the calamities and worries of being an adult.

3. **DON'T BE AFRAID TO GET DIRTY**
   Play in the rain, stomp in a puddle, make a mud pie and be carefree and worry-free while doing it. I know people that carry rain boots, a poncho, and an umbrella in their car at all times - just in case they get caught in the rain. What if you get caught in the rain? Is it the end of the world? Would your life change so drastically if you happened to get wet? Experience life hands on. It may be a little wet or a lot dirty, but the satisfaction of the experience is worth it.

4. **Use your Imagination**

    Imagination is life for a child. They can get lost in make-believe for hours, and adults can benefit from it too. The next time something is really bothering you, take a few minutes and use your imagination to put yourself in a better place. Close your eyes for a few minutes, imagine yourself on a beach. If you are worried about a presentation coming up, imagine yourself knocking it out of the park at work. Pretending actually has the potential to help you achieve your goals because you are seeing it and speaking it, which increases the likelihood of getting it or completing it. Use your imagination to put your life on a path of positivity.

Life, including yours, is meant to be fun and playful and carefree. Open your mind, body, and actions up to playing like a child and putting fun back into your daily life. The results will include a better life for you and a better version of you.

The Miscellaneous

16

Be a Helping Hand to Others

•

There is no greater feeling than helping others grow and succeed.

•

16: BE A HELPING HAND TO OTHERS

While the world may put emphasis on self, there is still a lot to be gained by giving support and being a helping hand to others. That does not mean you should neglect yourself or give everything and save nothing for you. Instead, it means do not be afraid to provide assistance to a friend in need (if you can) and be intentional in your actions to do things for others you may not know.

I've always been a kind person, but as I aged and witnessed people become homeless after a house fire, staying at homeless shelters to escape an abusive relationship, or struggling to find money to pay for life necessities after being laid off without notice, I realized that helping others isn't optional, it's mandatory. Why? Because any of these things just mentioned could happen to me at any given moment. The year leading to turning 30, I embarked on a personal campaign that I named 30x30. The objective of this campaign was to complete 30 kind acts before I turned 30. The acts did not have to be expensive acts or of large scale, but merely a genuine kind act for anyone – family, friend, or stranger. While I did not achieve the desired outcome for the campaign (I ended up with 21 of 30 at the end at the year), I learned a lot about myself, others, and how being helpful can truly go a long way. The feeling of helping others is unique to itself and you never know how your gesture of kindness and helping someone can affect them. One of my favorite quotes is by Oprah Winfrey, and it is, "Helping others is the way we help ourselves." Helping isn't about giving money because a lot of my 30x30 acts didn't involve money. They involved giving time, ideas, energy, or even just a listening ear. Helping others allows you to acquire new knowledge about yourself and understand others through their lives, and learning always leads to a better version of you.

THE MISCELLANEOUS

Here are some additional reasons why being a helping hand to others allows you to grow into the best version of you:

1. **INCREASES LIFE SATISFACTION**
   Life becomes more meaningful when you take the time to help others. It provides a sense of significance, improves moods, and reduces stress. Knowing that you have done a great deed to make another's life just a little bit better gives you a sense of accomplishment. Life is a little more satisfactory because you have made a positive difference. By helping others, I connect with people in ways that I never would and connecting with people creates positive bonds, stronger communities, and ultimately a happier society.

2. **INCREASES HAPPINESS**
   During the times when I am helping others, I feel happier. It genuinely feels good to know that me, little ol' Kendra, is contributing to making someone else's life a little bit better. Being a helping hand gives you that warm fuzzy feeling on the inside, the one that makes you smile, feel good, and want to do more of whatever it is that is giving you that feeling. That is the type of feeling that I want to have every day if I can. I know that might not be realistic but I definitely want to intentionally do things that will contribute to me feeling that type of happiness more frequently.

3. **GOOD FOR YOU OVERALL**
   Being a helping hand to others is a good thing for you in general. When you are spending time being helpful to others, you feel less stressed and less anxious. You feel better about yourself and are more hopeful. When I help others, I am less worried about my problems and

my level of gratitude is higher. I want to include my family and friends to experience this also, so I am inviting you to do things with me for others. It is contagious and it's something that you find yourself wanting to share with others.

It's simple. If you want to feel good, do good, and that includes being a helping hand to others. Allow yourself to be a blessing to others, and in return, others will be a blessing to you.

17

Engage in Continuous Learning

•

Just as the body requires nourishment to perform, the mind needs knowledge to continue to work at its full capacity. Ensure that you nourish your mind.

•

17: ENGAGE IN CONTINUOUS LEARNING

From the moment we are born, our brains are learning. Those first few years of life, from birth – age 5, our brain is operating on a genius level of learning everything that it comes into contact with – colors, sounds, smells, words, tastes, and everything imaginable. When the right things are placed into the mind during those critical years, a person can be set up for a successful life early on. Then something happens. As we age and go through the years of standardized schooling, we begin to hear students say things like, "I hate school" or "Learning is boring" and "I don't like to read or do math." By the time high school graduation comes along, there are some students with a mindset of, "I have met the requirements of the law, I will be satisfied if I never go to school again or never read another book in my life." I agree that college or classroom learning isn't fitting for everyone or necessary to lead a great life, but learning is essential to your very existence. Learning is a continuous, life-long endeavor for every single person, and those who strive to become the best version of themselves actively seek to add knowledge absorption to their daily lives.

Life and the major components in it are forever changing. You are forever changing. If you are the exact same way that you were 10 years ago and in the exact same place, I am going to question the progress that you claim to have made and the person that you are because you should be growing with age and changing right along with the times. What comes along with change? Learning. Changes in your career, changes in your personal life, changes in technology, changes in government laws and regulations - all require you to learn something new. A life without change is impossible, which means a life without continuous learning is unacceptable.

THE MISCELLANEOUS

You cannot be the best version of you if you are being left behind, and that is what happens when you avoid learning new skills. I absolutely love seeing older people working computers, taking selfies, and doing things that are deemed to be for the younger generations. This is a clear demonstration that these older individuals are accepting of what is becoming the norm of today's society and were willing to learn something new. I try to learn something new every single day of my life – whether it is something big or something small. Some days I may just learn a new vocabulary word. Other days, I may spend hours reading a book or watching tutorials on YouTube. In spite of the amount of time or effort, I am still learning. That new vocabulary word may come in handy in an important document or conversation with someone. That book I am reading may spark new ideas that can be useful in my life. That tutorial I watched may allow me to save money by doing something myself instead of paying another person or a big business. All of these things are made possible because I decided to continue learning. In addition, the confidence felt when you learn something and can execute it flawlessly as if you have known this all of your life is unparalleled. When I am speaking and use a new vocabulary word in the correct context and with the correct pronunciation, I feel like I am unstoppable. I ask myself how can you be anything but great when you can use the word mellifluous in your everyday diction. I know the saying goes, "You can't teach an old dog new tricks," but if that dog wants to remain relevant and keep significance, then there is no way around it except to learn new tricks. If not, time will continue and that same dog will be left sitting somewhere alone wishing they had taken time to learn. A prime example of this is adjusting in a work environment. Sometimes you have people that have been doing something a certain way for a very long time, and one day someone comes along and offers a newer, quicker way to do a task. The original person does not want to hear, let alone learn the new idea because this is not how it has always been done. It doesn't matter how much time, energy, or money it will save. These people will never be able to reach their full potential. These people will never be their best version.

Continuous learning means that you motivate yourself to acquire new knowledge, and you seek out new competencies that will magnify the understanding you already have and develop new skill sets that support your life journey and future opportunities. Knowledge and the ability to learn new things are more accessible now than any other time before. Technology has put an insurmountable amount of information at your fingertips; all you have to do is to tap into it. If you choose to not take advantage of this, do not be surprised when others surpass you. Do not be upset when you remain stagnant. Do not blame others when you are unable to elevate into a better version of you. Instead, help yourself navigate the inevitable life changes by armoring yourself with the greatest fuel for your mind, knowledge, and allow yourself to become the best you - a continuously learning you.

18

Have Intentional Friendships

•

The best friendships maintain an equal balance of give and take. If one person is doing more than the other, it becomes a seesaw with one side that never gets off the ground.

•

18: HAVE INTENTIONAL FRIENDSHIPS

"Friends! How many of us have them?" No seriously, take a brief moment and consider how many friends you have. Not Facebook friends, but real life, genuine friends. Is your number as high or low as you thought? Life is built around friendships. We are taught from a very young age that we should have friends. My son is only 2, but he still calls other kids in his room at his daycare his friends. This concept continues through grade school to high school to college and adulthood. Friendships are a vital part of life and who you are, which is why you must be intentional with your friendships. Having a large number of friends means absolutely nothing if all of those people are only taking away from your life and adding no value. The best friendships are those that support being the best version of you - where you are intentional about being a good friend and the receiving person reciprocates that same energy to you.

For many years in my 20s, I wanted to have a lot of friends. I would accept Facebook friend requests from anybody that sent me one, and I would put just as much effort into requesting to be friends with random people. I would ensure that I wrote Happy Birthday on your wall, and honestly spent entirely too much energy trying to keep up with people who really didn't care about me just so I could say they were my friend. Do you want to know how many people are really your friend or care about your well-being? Go off the grid. In 2015, when I was going through some of my toughest trials, I deactivated my Facebook page, deleted everything off my Instagram, and kept my cell phone off for a good part of every day. I didn't want to face my reality or others concerning my reality. I just knew that people were going to be concerned about me and what happened to me. I was completely wrong. Most of the people that I thought were my "friends" did not bother to call or text. I would turn on my phone and no messages would come through and there wouldn't be any voicemails. But there were a few wonderful souls who went above and beyond - leaving items in my mailbox, sending balloons to my job, emailing me at my job to check on me, messaging my sister on her Facebook page to ask what happened to my Facebook page, and that's when I understood who my real friends truly were. I finally understood what true friendship was and decided to be intentional with my friendships going forward.

Intentional friendships assist you in being the best version of you because these friendships successfully uplift you, motivate you, love you, and genuinely want to see you at your best. Intentional friendships do not require speaking every day, but when you do speak, the conversations consist of truth and honesty. Intentional friendships intentionally serve a purpose in your life. Becoming the best version of you requires you to assess your friendships and the role they play in your life. You must be brutally honest with yourself about these people and the value they are contributing. If you are always the one calling, always the one checking on them, always there when they need you, but those same activities are not being given in return, that friendship is one-sided and you need to cut the line. If your friends don't call you out on your craziness, look out for your best interest at all times, or tell you when you are making poor decisions, they are not your real friends, and keeping them in your life isn't helping you on your life journey. I know it is difficult to remove individuals who have been in your life for a long time. I have experienced dissolved friendships after 20 years of memories and laughs, but I had to accept the fact that our lives were on different paths and that holding on was more tragic than letting go. But just the same as some friendships were lost, new friendships were gained, and as they developed, these friendships were and are intentional in my life and aiding me on my life journey. These are the friendships that I need and want. These are the friendships that you must strive for in your life.

19

Don't Take It Personal

●

Your life is your center. Never grant another person the power to disrupt it.

●

19: DON'T TAKE IT PERSONAL

How many times has someone done something to you and it automatically ruined your mood and your day? How often do you find yourself in an unhappy state because of something happening that was beyond your control or the actions of another person? Many times, we allow our mental states, our emotions, and our days to be impacted by others because we have taken something personally. People have made decisions in their lives that may or may not directly affect us and their decisions have created an effect on our lives. Now we are very upset, hurt, and discombobulated. We have taken it personally and permitted our life and our peace to be disturbed. How crazy is that? Your life is yours, and it is up to you to keep it running smoothly with limited stress. This only happens if you are not taking things personally. If everything that everyone else does bothers you to the point where it is creating lasting negativity in your life, you have essentially handed over the keys to your happiness and your life to them. Sometimes this person might be a stranger. Your life is too vital to leave in the hands of a stranger. If someone cuts you off in traffic, don't take it personally. If someone takes your parking space at the mall during holiday shopping, don't take it personally. If a co-worker gets the promotion that you wanted and worked to get for months, don't take it personally.

Why shouldn't you take things personally? Most importantly, because whatever you are taking personally has absolutely nothing to do with you. The actions people take are their own decisions, and they do it because they want to. They may try to pawn off their decisions as being because of you, but the reality is they wanted to. A spouse cheated because they wanted to. A friend borrowed money and didn't repay it because they wanted to. Therapists consistently tell people to not blame themselves for what others have done or are doing. When you accept the concept that nothing others do is because of you, you will no longer allow yourself to be upset or your life disrupted because of them. You will not take things personally. Your space will not be uneasy, and that is when your best self shines through. Others' stupidity or mediocrity will not phase you, and you will no longer be a victim to choices that you did not make. You are free to choose what will impact your happiness and what will not. You can truly focus on what you control, your own life.

I have struggled, and still sometimes struggle, with taking things personally. Some of the worst times of my life were plagued with additional stress because I was taking everything personally. Every time someone did something I didn't like or said something that I didn't want to hear, it would send me into a downward spiral. I was on a daily emotional rollercoaster because I was blaming myself and making myself the victim of what everyone else was doing. No one should live that way, and there is no way that you can be your best when you are emotionally unbalanced.

It is imperative to master the idea of not taking things personally. I understand that it's highly unlikely to never take anything personally, but if you actively practice it, I can firmly say that you will find yourself less annoyed with people and the minuscule things of life. With time, you will take less and less things personally, and be able to use your energy on the positive things of your life.

20

You Can't (and Won't) Please Everybody

•

A life spent trying to please others is a life wasted.

•

20: YOU CAN'T (AND WON'T) PLEASE EVERYBODY

How many times in a day do you concern yourself with pleasing people? Seriously, take a moment and think about it. For most of us, myself included, we are consistently internally asking questions like, "Will they like this post?" or "Should I wear this outfit?" or even "Will they like what I say?" in an attempt to please others. A good part of our lives is spent trying to please other individuals and ensure that we are liked by the masses. Is this a bad thing? Not necessarily. It is human nature to want to be liked, almost like a fundamental need. We are built to interact with others and not experience life alone. We must be liked by someone – that is a part of building friendships and relationships. The important thing is to not become obsessed with trying to be liked or pleasing others to the point of denying your true self, pretending to be something that you are not, and holding yourself back from unleashing your full potential. Why? Because you cannot and will not be able to please everybody. No matter how pretty you are, no matter how much good you do, no matter how much money you have and spend, there will always be somebody who doesn't like you and probably for no other reason than they just don't have to. To live a life that includes being your best self, you must accept that you cannot and will not be able to please everybody, and that is okay.

Today's society has made it hard to NOT want to please people. Especially when likes, views, subscribers, etc., have now been equated to money, lifestyles, and livelihoods. Nonetheless, it is extremely unhealthy to live your life in a way where everything you do is for the approval or pleasing of others. Instead of focusing your energy on pleasing others, strive to please yourself and recognize that the individuals who are truly for you and meant to be in your life will be there. And not because they care about being pleased, but because they care about being a part of your life and your awesomeness. Please yourself so that you sleep well at night and know that you are doing your best. Be proud of the person you are becoming, so that you are creating the dialogue for your life that you want.

In those times when you feel yourself slipping back into a people-pleasing mindset, gently remind yourself (like I do from time to time) that your worth is not tied to likes and does not need any approval. You are wonderfully made whether a post gets 10 likes, 100 likes, or 1 million likes. You are already worthy just because of who you are and the person you are becoming. Your growth and your drive are more than enough.

Not wanting to please everybody is a concept that will take time to master. There will be plenty of times when you will once again find yourself asking questions about who will or won't like this or if something is enough for so and so. As I have been writing this very book, I have found myself wondering if this will be interesting to anybody or will people even want to read it? In spite of those fears, I have kept pushing through because I need to do this for me. I want to be an author, and I want to help people enjoy their lives with success and being the best version of themselves. Even if a single person doesn't read this book, I will still be pleased and proud of myself. Be the best you without the worry of pleasing everybody.

The Val-"You"s

21

Mind Your Mind

•

Clear your mind for only the things that matter and your life will be free.

•

21: MIND YOUR MIND

Think about the number of different things that cross your mind on a daily basis. What about the number of things that you need to accomplish or address? If your days are anything like mine, that number is astronomical. It seems like I am always in "multi-task" mode, and even when I am actually working on a single thing, my mind and brain are still doing so much more. Some of the things that are on my mind have been there for days, weeks, months, years even – and they are not showing any signs of dissipating any time soon. I feel this way quite frequently, and it can be extremely frustrating. Frustrating to the point where I don't want to do anything or to the point where I have headaches or to the point where I must unload some of these things off my mind; especially the negative things that are hoarding space in my brain. Completing a regular brain dump aids in keeping you happy and your mind free to focus on what your life is supposed to be.

So what is a brain dump? Well, it is exactly what it sounds like. It requires taking everything that is currently taking up all of the space in your brain and dumping out. It's the release of all of your thoughts - everything that you have built up, are worried about, that you need to do, that you are feeling questionable about… EVERYTHING is released. There are several ways you can do this – I always like to go old school and put pen to paper and write out my actual thoughts. However, if that's too archaic for you, feel free to type them out in a note on your phone or put them in an email to yourself. It doesn't matter how you do it, as long as you are dumping all of these things in a place that you can actually and physically see. Once all of these things are written out and in a visible place, you can see first-hand how much stuff is really on your mind and create a plan for how to handle them. You can take time to organize all of these thoughts and free your mind from a lot of clutter.

Why is a brain dump such a great tool? I've said it before, and I will say it again - the mind is such a vital part of your life. Everything starts with your thoughts; when your mind is cluttered, so is your life. Let's be honest, most people (myself included) tend to procrastinate and let tasks (big and small) build up. We tend to overthink and allow things to stay on our minds for longer than their expiration date. Then one day we feel overwhelmed by ALL of the things that are going on and wonder why we can't accomplish things, have headaches, or are unable to sleep. Because your mind is full, and at this time, a brain dump is absolutely necessary.

There is no right or wrong time to conduct a brain dump, but you should definitely look for the signs of when your brain is getting too full. I like to do a weekly brain dump to try and avoid getting to the point where my brain is overloaded. Plus, conducting one on a weekly basis allows me to do a sort of deep cleansing of my mind and give me a fresh start to a week. Of course, there are random times when it's a crazy day and a brain dump may be required, but the key is determining your triggers and noticing when you are feeling overwhelmed – becoming self-aware (which is a great trait to have). In those moments, make the time to physically write out what's going on and take a moment to release.

22

Sweat, Smile, Repeat

•

Exercise is therapy for your body. Indulge in it and allow your body to reap the rewards.

•

22: SWEAT, SMILE, REPEAT

It's a common fact that exercise is great for the body. It doesn't matter if you are overweight, underweight, or perfectly proportioned according to medical standards – exercise provides benefits that can help you live longer. I have always been of petite stature with a slim frame, which has always made people assume that I did not need to work out or that I was in a good, healthy condition, and honestly, for a good part of my life (especially in my 20s), I thought the same thing. However, as the latter part of my 20s came, I found myself being winded doing even the simplest of tasks or having work health screenings tell me that my cholesterol levels were in the heart attack range. I quickly realized that even I needed to exercise and be more healthy and fitness conscious.

This mindset was even stronger after experiencing pregnancy and facing the reality that some parts of my body would never be the same as they once were. I started doing some light weight lifting and exercises, and it felt great! Yes, I was sore sometimes, and yes, the day after had its pains, but it still felt good. And not only just physically, but mentally and emotionally. As I continued on the journey of becoming the best version of me, I researched more about exercising, and it quickly became evident that exercising is indeed an important factor of being the best version of you. While it may not be your favorite thing to do, the value that it provides to your life is undeniable. This body is yours - your best self resides in it, and it is the only body you have to live this life. Therefore, you must take the time to ensure it stays in the best shape, top condition, and capable of harnessing all of your greatness. Exercising is an essential way to assist with that.

THE VAL-YOUs

There are many benefits to getting up and exercising, but here are four ways that it helps you in becoming and being the best you:

1. **REDUCES INSOMNIA**

   When you exercise and stay active on a consistent basis, it improves your sleeping patterns. The body is a well-oiled machine, and just like it needs exercise, it needs adequate rest to rejuvenate. It is the balance to your exercise. The sleep after a day of exercise and a good shower is some of the best sleep that you will ever have. Good, fulfilling sleep leads to a better you because you wake up refreshed, energized, and ready to take on a new day.

2. **ENERGY ENHANCER**

   Has this ever happened to you? You feel too tired to work out and really don't want to go but you are committed to it and decide to go anyway. Then once you work out, you feel energized and ready to take on the world. That is because exercise actually enhances your energy levels. When that blood gets flowing and you are doing what the body actually needs and wants, you have more energy. More energy provides you with an opportunity to do more things.

3. **CONFIDENCE BOOSTER**

   I haven't always had the best confidence. The amount of short jokes and too skinny references that I have endured in my life is more than I want to acknowledge. However, when I started working out, I truly started to have more confidence in my shape and figure. Yes, I may be short and petite, but those abs don't just appear on their own. That's a product of hard work and dedication. Those feelings helped me embrace myself and support becoming a better me. When you exercise and you are seeing the results of your labor, your confidence goes up. You feel good about yourself and your body. Confidence in yourself and with yourself is critical to being the best version of you.

4. **HAPPINESS**

    Exercise makes you happy, and not just the concept of being happy but actual happiness. Exercising has been connected to releasing dopamine into your body, and dopamine is a chemical that is associated with transmitting happiness to the brain. By exercising you are actively supporting dopamine production and creating additional happiness and pleasure in your life.

Make a commitment to add a little more exercise to your life. Pick an activity that you like and start with once or twice a week. If you enjoy it, add more days. If not, try a different activity. The key is to give your body the workout it needs – Sweat, Smile, Repeat!

23

Find your Spiritual Strength

•

Attune yourself to something beyond the physical. Connect to the innermost part of you.

•

23: FIND YOUR SPIRITUAL STRENGTH

I grew up in the church. My parents ensured that we were instilled with a good foundation around God and religion, but I truly didn't tap into my spiritual side until my later 20s when I felt like my life was falling apart. This is when I really had to determine what I believed in. Don't get me wrong – all of my life (well as far as I can remember), I have always believed in God, known right from wrong, believed in a higher power and prayed, but it was more because it was what I was taught, not what I felt.

When I was in my darkest times, I consistently asked God why he was doing this to me. I could not fathom what I had done in my life span to have such pain and travesties bestowed upon me. Was I a perfect saint? No, not even close. I had my flaws just like the next person. I made bad decisions. I acted based on anger sometimes, but I also wasn't an evil person. I wasn't purposely plotting against others or maliciously seeking harm or destruction in the lives of people, so why was I being put through so much? "Why me?" was the question consistently running through my thoughts. I concluded that maybe I was not fit for life or maybe I just couldn't cut it.

Looking back now, I realize that I was completely lost spiritually. I didn't have a real solid belief in a higher power. I did not have a connection that would remind me that storms do pass, life is worth living for so many reasons, and that my purpose and plan is greater than any tribulation. I did not have the spiritual strength to help me get through tough times nor the faith to remain positive and hold on since trials are only temporary. In recent years, I have intentionally positioned myself to have a spiritual connection with God that provides strength when I'm weak, clarity when I'm confused, and love when all I feel is hurt. This connection puts me in better spirits on a regular basis and allows me to be a better person because I know that my spiritual strength can get me through anything if I use it to its full capacity and trust it wholeheartedly. Attending church regularly, prayer, meditation, reading and studying all have contributed to me getting to this state and I am overjoyed to have found my spiritual strength to lean on as I journey through life. But it is not a one-stop shop, maintaining this strength requires consistent learning, studying, and understanding. I continue to feed my soul and exude love to guarantee that my spiritual strength is maintained. It's just like a muscle that requires work to maintain its strength and size, and being the best version of me includes the continuous working of that muscle.

Take some time to find your spiritual center and determine what you connect to. Build your spiritual strength and use it as your armor as you go through the stages of life. Find your tribe of spiritual individuals whose beliefs match yours and are willing to fight a spiritual battle alongside you if necessary. I am forever grateful that I have praying family and friends who are always willing to pray with me or for me. Read, learn, and expand your knowledge base. Set a routine that works for you and allows you to focus on your spiritual connection. Your soul, your spiritual center, or whatever you call it, is an essential part of you and aids in you becoming and living as your best self.

24

Manage your Emotions

•

The ability to control the emotions within you is the feat that changes everything about the way you live life. Revel in this strength.

•

24: MANAGE YOUR EMOTIONS

Too many times, we have emotional overreactions. You know when you get angry and all you see is red and revenge. Or maybe you are sad about something and cry or mope for days. It seems that society has made it "approved" to act irrationally due to emotional overreactions. How frequently do you hear statements about how someone will react or what they will do if a certain situation were to happen to them? I am going to kill my man or woman if they ever cheat on me, or put me in jail now because if this or that happens to me, I am going to war. They are already planning to emotionally overreact before anything has even occurred. How often do you hear or read stories about people or companies making a comment, post, or email in the heat of the moment that has created an uproar and resulted in undesired consequences? Thinking from a non-emotional standpoint, would any of those reactions solve the problem or make you a better person? Will they make the situation better or easier to cope with? I am no stranger to emotional overreactions. I have bleached boyfriend's clothes, jumped on moving vehicles, chased people in vehicles, cried for what seemed like forever, just laid and didn't move for days – all because my emotions were controlling me, literally. Reminiscing on previous situations, I don't think I ever really had a good grasp of how to properly manage my emotions until recently, and even now, it is still a battle to not let things get out of control. I recall instances of rage and wanting to fight people including family members because of the anger that I allowed to consume me. I recollect extreme situations in past relationships because I was so hurt or upset and allowed my emotions to take me to a place of hysteria to the point where I was putting myself and others' lives in harm's way. Those were not smart decisions and I wasn't being my best self in those cases.

THE VAL-YOUs

The concept to grasp is, you must be responsible and accountable for your emotions. You must ask yourself – do I manage my emotions or do my emotions manage me? How many times have you said after the fact that your emotions got the best of you? Realistically, in life, we are going to go through a plethora of emotions all the time. Joy to fear, anger to sadness, hurt to love to happiness, and there is no real manual or compass to help you live with them on a daily basis. However, it is counterproductive to suppress your emotions and also not in your best interest to allow them to control you completely. The best answer is the happy medium of accepting your emotions and then managing them.

I understand that managing your emotions is very tricky and sometimes seems like an impossible task, but the first step is to acknowledge that you do have a variety of emotions and it is ok to have these emotions – it's life. Once that has been accepted, you are on your way to effective emotional management. Here are a few reminders that can help as you strive to manage your emotions:

1. **YOU ARE NOT YOUR EMOTIONS**
   While emotions are very strong and very impactful, recognize that you are NOT your emotions. You are just a person, like everyone else, with morals, values, and thoughts who also have emotions that are triggered by circumstances and situations in life on an on-going basis. Succumbing to the misconception that you are indeed your emotions is the quickest way to allow them to control you. Statements such as "I'm just an angry person" or "That's Me, I'm So and So" are mere excuses to allow that emotion to run rampant. Separation of the emotion that you are currently feeling and who you are at your core helps to not allow the

emotion to dictate your actions and behavior.

2. **EMOTIONS AREN'T BAD**
   Somewhere along the line, we were taught that emotions are good or bad. Think about it? Being happy or joyful is thought to be a good thing, yet being fearful or scared is thought to be a bad thing. Despite what others may say or what society deems as good or bad, emotions are neither positive nor negative – they are just emotions. When you think of them without a positive or negative connotation, it releases the misconception that you shouldn't embrace a certain emotion and allows you to freely accept whatever the emotion is, thus increasing the likelihood of managing it without overreacting.

3. **THERE IS ALWAYS A CHOICE**
   Don't believe the hype, you always have a choice. Just because you are feeling a particular emotion doesn't mean that you have to act a certain way. Feeling angry does not mean that you have to break things, cuss out people, or act irrationally, just like feeling happy does not mean that you have to be overly smiley. You can cry when you are sad but it is ok if you don't. You are in control and have the ability to decide how you will act in response to what emotion you have felt. You may not always be able to choose your emotions but you can always choose how to react to them. There is always a choice and you have the responsibility to choose a response that will help you versus hurt you.

Take control of your emotions and manage them in an effective manner that will aid you in life. Scream when frustrated, cry when hurt – it is all ok, but make sure that in those instances when your emotions are strongest and you feel them deeply that you do not allow your judgment to be clouded and emotional overreacting to put you in a place that will be more harmful than helpful in the long run. Remember, we will experience a lot of emotions on a daily basis, so make an effort to manage them and realize that your true strength is being able to control yourself despite what the emotion is making you feel.

25

Embrace Your Growth

•

Release the concept of fearing change and embrace the idea that from your growth, a new, improved, version of you will arise.

•

25: EMBRACE YOUR GROWTH

For the most part, we as humans, don't like change and growth. Why? Because we like to be comfortable. We like the ease of been familiar with situations. I openly admit that growth has always scared me to an extent. Going from middle school to high school, going from high school to college, graduating from college and having to be an adult in the "real world," becoming a wife, and definitely becoming a mom. I was a nervous wreck thinking about the pending task of being responsible for an entire human when I was pregnant. I spent days thinking about what if I did something wrong or what if something happened because of my shortcomings. But every single time, even though I was frightened of what was coming with the new aspect and fearful of failing, I also always understood that the pending growth was absolutely necessary. Right now, writing this book is growth for me and it's scary. Being an author is unknown territory for me. I don't know if this book will be a success. I wonder if anybody will want to buy it, but regardless of all of that, I am determined to complete this goal and the growth I will receive from this experience will add to who I am and help me on my life journey. Embrace your growth. Revel in your strength to change with life. The reality is that growth is tough, but it is also a life necessity. Without change and without growth, you are limiting yourself from becoming who you are destined to be and doing yourself a grave injustice.

I know it's scary for your mindset to change and your behaviors to shift - it's almost like you have to relearn your own self, but it is a good thing. Thinking back to my mindset at age 21 versus age 25 versus age 30 – there are major differences. Even now, I find myself learning more about myself as I have to choose between doing something for myself or my son. Now I make decisions only after weighing all options – something I would have never done in my younger years. I always find it comical when people say, "Well, you changed." I have to politely remind them "Yes, I have. That is what you are supposed to do." I shouldn't think the same way that I did when I was 16. I'm in my 30s now and lived through various situations from depression to failed relationships to unexpected deaths. Those things change you. Those situations change your views and your thought process. I am supposed to grow. Think about it, as we age, we are placed in different situations that derive from the actions of previous situations. Without embracing growth and learning from the previous, you will consistently find yourself in a vicious cycle of repeating the same actions, some of which may be mistakes. You are bigger than that and you are meant for more.

Accept your growth because it is vital for your success and happiness. We are on this journey to become the best version of ourselves and embracing the change and growth grants us the means for how to get there. This personal growth releases the sentiment of self-centeredness which plagues so many and aids in promoting more love in the world. As you age, your world expands to include so many others along with new opportunities. Embracing your growth makes you fit to handle all of the new possibilities that are coming your way. Live intentionally in this moment and welcome the joy and peace that comes from accepting your growth and change. Your evolution into your best version is required and near.

The Daily Reminders

26

It's Ok to Say "No!"

•

Saying no makes room to be able to say yes to the things that you truly want in your life.

•

26: IT'S OK TO SAY NO

Life Strategy #16 spoke on being a helping hand to others and taking time to assist when possible, but what you also need to know is that helping others should never be to the extent that it becomes detrimental to you. It is wonderful to help others, but at the same time, you must take care of yourself. You cannot pour into someone else if your glass is empty. Therefore, a concept to master includes understanding and implementing the idea that it is ok to say no to others.

We all know that saying no is not the easiest task; especially if you are a natural born helper like me. You just want to help others whenever you can because you love it. Others are unable to say no because they want to be liked or accepted or pleasing. Either way, while it may be extremely difficult, it is critically important to be able to say no. Too many times in life, I have found myself doing things that I really did not want to do because I was afraid to say no. Burning myself out, losing sleep, and stressing myself in order to be helpful to others because I said yes when I really wanted to say no. I know people that have accepted jobs that they didn't want to, gone on trips with people that they didn't want to, even going as far as marrying someone that they had doubts about because of the inability to say no. Not saying no has the capability to impact your life in many ways, so before you say yes when you want to say no, think of the big picture of your life. It's crazy how one small and simple word can hold so much power in one's life. Therefore, you must conquer the skill to purposely use this world and manage the power it yields.

Most people don't want to hurt someone's feelings or seem selfish by saying no, but you also can not neglect your own

THE DAILY REMINDERS

feelings or needs to accommodate others. When you are saying yes when you actually want to say no, you tend to find yourself creating feelings of resentment and anger, as well as thoughts of regret because you could be doing something else. The result is you will be in a negative headspace while pretending to be happy and cheery about whatever you are doing. Think about how draining that sounds – all because you were unable to say no. Don't place yourself in a predicament to have negative thoughts, anxiety, or displeasure. Just be firm and remember that it is ok to say no. However, if you are like me, the extreme ultimate giver, and still have a difficult time getting into the rhythm of saying no, here are four tips to assist with getting into the habit of saying no:

1. **GIVE YOURSELF TIME TO PROCESS**

   Being too eager to respond tends to result in a quick yes instead of a delayed no. When asked to do something and you aren't sure if you really want to or even have the time, it is perfectly ok to say, "Let me get back to you" and allow yourself a window to truly contemplate whether you will say yes or no. If the requestor really wants you to do something, they will respect your wishes to get back to them. If they don't and find someone else, then they really didn't want you to begin with and just needed someone to fill the need. It is not mandatory that you give a response immediately. Take the time to choose yes or no.

2. **BE COMPLETELY HONEST WITH YOURSELF**

   Being honest, especially with yourself, is essential and one of the hardest things to do. When you are asked to do something, ask yourself if you actually want to do it. If your honest answer is, "I don't know" or "No," then you know what the response to the person should be.

Honesty is the best approach to everything, so be sure to employ it with yourself first and say no if that's your truth.

3. **START SMALL AND WORK YOUR WAY UP**
   Do you ever find yourself taking sales calls that you don't want to be on? What about upsizing at fast food restaurants when you really did not want to but said yes anyway? Start building your ability to say no by saying no to the little things such as upgrading sizes at Burger King, buying accessories at the cell phone store or stopping to talk to people selling items in the middle of the outlet mall when you are in a hurry. Saying no to the little things and strangers will help you build your confidence so that when the time comes when you want to say no to a close friend or family member, you will have the ability to.

4. **TRUST YOUR INTUITION**
   Your intuition is the first indicator that something is not right and normally is correct. If your intuition is telling you that you don't want to do something or you shouldn't do something, trust it and say no. Sometimes our feelings can get lost in translation when we are trying to make decisions, but your intuition is always there and for a great reason. Listen to your gut. Trust your intuition, and only say yes if you truly know it's right and it feels right.

27

Take a Moment for Yourself

•

Only in a place of true tranquility can one release regrets of the past, distractions of the present, and worries of the future, to reach a place of absolute clarity.

•

27: TAKE A MOMENT FOR YOURSELF

Most people spend the entirety of their day on the go. First thing in the morning, we start by watching the news, checking emails, scrolling social media, rushing to get ready for work, and the cycle continues throughout the day. We go from home to work to picking up kids to some practice and back home. The entire time they are awake, they are in motion. Is this you? Is that how you live your life? Let's stop and think about something. How often do you take time out to just be? To be still and present in the current moment doing nothing more – no phone, no emails, no talking – completely nothing. I recognize that you are busy and there is always something that needs to be done, or a battle that needs to be fought, or a fire that requires your attention, but even with all of that, you must take a moment to have stillness for yourself.

Every day you should have a small timeout to "Just Be" and enjoy a moment for you. It doesn't have to be a long time, it can be 5 minutes, 15 minutes, an hour, or longer. It can come at the start of the day, in the middle, or at the end, but no matter the length of time or when, it is absolutely necessary to take time to break away and focus on yourself. This moment is critical for becoming the best version of you.

I fell victim to this in my 20s. Working multiple jobs, in school, and still attempting to be the cool girl and go out with friends and hang with family. My mindset was "I'm in my 20s, I can do it all." And indeed, I was doing it all, but I was not my best self or even close. I was operating at less than 100% daily – carrying worries from day to day and making excuses for why this was ok. In retrospect, if I had dedicated a little bit of time to myself, to just think, relax, and pray, I know for a fact that I

THE DAILY REMINDERS

would have made different decisions in my life.

Because life is busy and full of decisions, studies have proven that decisions are best made when one is in the clearest mental space, making personal time a top priority. Taking a moment for yourself every day allows you the opportunity to experience a little bit of tranquility in the ever chaotic world that we live in. This moment to yourself can be used to pray, meditate, relax, or do whatever gives you a sense of peace and a chance to release all of your worries, stresses, and thoughts of the day. Taking a moment for yourself shows that you value yourself, your time, and your sanity. You recognize it is ok to be alone and love yourself in your solidarity.

Your daily moment is specific and unique to you. It is your personal chance to slow down and enjoy every day of your life. Use it to decompress and detach yourself from all of the distractions of the world such as beeping tones, flashing lights, and vibrations that hold us hostage throughout the day and night. Rediscover your goals every day and renew the passion to reach your full potential in this life. There are no rules for your personal time. In this moment, do whatever you feel you want to and need to. Breathe deeply, scream loudly, cry if necessary, and realign yourself to the authentic you. Every day we face the world, it is full of people and things trying to strip you of your joy. You must not allow it. Whatever things that you feel you must do every day will more than likely still be there tomorrow, so make sure you are your best by taking a moment for yourself.

.

28

Always Do Your Best

•

Life is too short for mediocrity.
Always do your best.

•

28: ALWAYS DO YOUR BEST

No matter what you are doing in life or where you are going, you should always do and give your best. When you always do your best, you spare yourself from asking questions like "what if" and "why not." You understand that despite the outcome, you gave and did the best that you could and if it didn't happen or work in your favor, then it just wasn't meant for you. When you live life always putting your best foot forward, there are no regrets or questions about what is or isn't for you. Every day, in every situation and every circumstance, always do your best - nothing more, nothing less.

Why would you really want to do something halfway or sub-par anyway? When you are not trying your best, you are wasting something that cannot be replaced or regained – your time! Doing your best affords you the ability to take pride and be satisfied with yourself and the time spent because you know that you gave it your all, and that is an awesome feeling.

Quite frequently these days, I am asked how I continue to manage when things in life fail. And my answer is always the same - because I tried my absolute best and had no regrets about what happened. I have no regrets in failed relationships, lost friendships, or unsuccessful projects. That is the absolute truth, but that wasn't always the case. For years, I would do things in an average manner and then question the results. I didn't always give my best in a job interview, but then would be mad that I didn't get the job. I didn't always do the best I could on exams in college, but then I would wonder if I would have passed a class the first time if I had actually tried to study instead of partying. Think of some things in life that you might say you regret or situations that you may have asked what if or why not… interviews, jobs, relationships, and schooling – did you always give your best to these things? Would things have been different if you did? You will never be able to alter the way someone else thinks, you are incapable of changing the way another acts, but you can always do your best and be at peace with what occurs in life when you do.

Always doing your best isn't as simple as it sounds. So many people get accustomed to doing just enough to get by. Here are a few additional reasons why doing your best contributes to you being the best version of you:

1. **PRIDE**

    There is an automatic sense of pride that you feel when you give and do your best. It's a feeling of fulfillment and a sense of accomplishment whether you win or lose, succeed or fail, simply because you gave it your best shot with everything that you could. Nothing is truly a loss if it is a result of you giving your best shot. You are able to hold your head up high and hone pride. I always love that final scene in the movie, Cool Runnings, when they walk across the finish line carrying their bobsled and everyone is clapping for them. The pride displayed in that scene is phenomenal. Despite them not winning their run, they gave it their very best and for that reason, they were the true winners.

2. **LEARNING MORE ABOUT YOURSELF**

    How can you determine what you are good or bad at if you never do your best? Are you a great swimmer? What about a great writer? You are incapable of truly learning what skills you have if you never do your best at anything. When you do your best, you are learning about yourself and what things come naturally to you. If you try something and give it your very best and it doesn't go the way that you would have liked, then maybe that activity is not for you. Always doing your best helps you identify your personal strengths and weaknesses.

3. **GROWTH – YOU GET BETTER**
   Doing your best allows you to identify your strengths, and now you can give your attention to getting better in that skill. That can only be done by doing your best. Athletes strive to break their last best record all the time. The fastest running time or number of points scored in a game is only broken by the athlete always doing their best in every race or game. Pushing yourself to the next level by always doing your best provides the opportunity for growth.

4. **OVERCOME FEAR OF FAILURE**
   Many don't give their best at something because of a fear of failing. If you never give your best to start, you have already failed. No matter the outcome, if you do your best, there is no failure and no regrets. Don't fear that you won't do as well as you want or you will automatically yield to that fear. Instead, stay in the current moment and try your very best. Don't set expectations and in the moment do your very best. This mindset has no place for your fear and removes it completely as you focus on the moment and your best - nothing more, nothing less.

Always doing your best is pertinent to being the best version of you. Investing your energy into the current moment and giving it your all is a practice that will aid you in improving your life. Always do your best, and you will be astonished by the results that follow. When you are not doing your best, you are not your best, plain and simple.

29

Giving is Living

•

When you begin to truly give, you will also begin to truly live. Giving is Living.

•

29: GIVING IS LIVING

It doesn't matter who you are, what you do, or where you are in life, you have something to give... something that someone else needs. It could be something free. It could be something minute. It could be something life-changing, but whatever it is, someone needs it, and you are destined to give it.

I have always been a giver. For as long as I can remember, I have been willing to go out of my way to provide for the needs of others. Some may say that I give too much. I have heard from plenty of people that I am too nice and too kind to people. But I say that there is no such thing. I give, not for an award, not for likes, not for recognition, but because I feel happy when I give. I get a sense of accomplishment and I want that feeling as often as possible. Giving is not about money or being seen doing good. It is about helping those in need and having a heart of love to do so whether they appreciate it or not.

It is refreshing to give and that feeling you have after giving is like nothing else. It reminds you and others that life isn't just about you, but everyone. Giving provides positive results for both the giver and the receiver, so don't shy away from giving or cause someone and yourself to miss their blessings because you chose not to give.

Critics may say that giving too much may result in people taking advantage of your generosity. My response to that is, who cares if they do? Your heart of giving will always prevail over anyone attempting to take advantage of your spirit. Do not worry about what they think or what they may be receiving from getting over on you. Instead, focus on the benefits you are gaining overall by actively participating in a life geared towards giving. The feeling of making a positive difference is one that everyone should experience – the happiest, most fulfilled people recognize this and seek to keep that feeling by continuously giving to others in spite of what others are giving in return. When you agree to give because it is fun, helpful, and most importantly, from a place of love, the rewards you will reap are astonishing. When you give, you live, and giving is a key to opening yourself to be the best you, the giving you, the living you.

30

Love Everybody, Everything, Every day

•

There is no greater power in the universe than the Power of Love – Love Unconditionally.

•

30: LOVE EVERYBODY, EVERYTHING, EVERY DAY

We started with Life Strategy #1 – Love Yourself and now at the end, we conclude with Life Strategy #30 - Love Everybody, Everything, Every day. To be the best you and live the best life, a successful life, you must do everything with LOVE. The purpose of life is LOVE – to live it, to give it, to be it … LOVE.

Forgive with Love, cry with Love, laugh with Love, make important decisions with Love, and live life to the best of your ability with LOVE! Frequently, we live in a place of hurt and we make decisions from a place of revenge. This means we act from a place of hate, and in turn, wonder why things never get better. Love is a universal currency, a concept that can be understood and accepted across all races, genders, continents, and languages. It is a critical component that has the capability to join individuals in a way that nothing else can. Everything is better. Everything grows with love, and love can change everything.

When you live a life of love, you recognize and accept that whatever happens, just happens. You are happier, more carefree, and able to go about life with less stress because you are not living a life of fear. Love is the true north of life, and when you use it as your compass, you will always end up at the appropriate destination. If you want to create a life with all of the values and attributes desired – kindness, genuineness, compassion, loyalty, joy, appreciation, you must plant seeds of love in everything you do. You are the creator of your life and everything in it; make the choice to live a life of love. You must strive to fight less and love more. Focus on the beauty of every moment in the present and expand your thoughts and feelings to push love into these moments. Be love, and allow it to lead you in your decisions.

When I thought I was failing in life, my love was at an all-time low. I only saw pain and hurt, and for that reason alone, life was so much harder and unpleasant. I couldn't fathom anyone else loving me because I was blinded by the hate being displayed by others. This blindness kept me in the dark for far too long. Love is not darkness. Love embodies light, and that light will guide you down the correct path in life. Love is hope and that hope reminds you that every day offers you something new. Love is faith and that faith is the firm belief in yourself and your purpose of life. Faith, Hope, and Love – the trinity of all existence... LIFE. Embed them in your soul as you move through your life journey.

So what's next? What should you start doing immediately? Start implementing more love into your life, into your daily activities - with your boss who doesn't appreciate the dedicated employee that you are, towards your ex who betrayed you and broke your heart, to the friend that you had a falling out with about something so minuscule that you don't even remember it, to the stranger who is in a hurry in the grocery store and cut you in the checkout line - every day in every way. Always remember, the basis of life is LOVE, and all things for your life begin and end with you.

Final Thoughts

Take a moment and think about your life. Reflect on the past, imagine the future, and open your eyes back in the present – your current reality. The time has arrived. You know what you need to do. All you have to do now is complete the actions to get it done. This book has provided you with the tools and knowledge necessary to cultivate your life. Now it is time for you to get to work to become the person you are meant to be and do that which you are meant to do.

My prayer is that you reach your goals, you fulfill your purpose, and you become the best you. I want everyone, you included, to be successful and win in life. We wake up every morning with a new chance to make a difference in our own lives and the lives of those around us. We must start taking advantage of this opportunity.

All we really have is right now. Yesterday is gone and tomorrow may never come. Right now is the moment that we can alter and create something that the world needs, something powered by love. It may seem hard and some days will be better than others, but it's all worth it and necessary to develop the true life for you as the best version of you. There is and will always be only one you, and you only get one chance at life. Therefore, strive to be the version you are destined to be. Find the courage to grow and become the best version of you. Thank you for reading, and I hope you enjoyed this book.

Be Kind, Be Generous, Be Loving,

About the Author

Success Advocate and Motivational Speaker, Kendra Logan, lives with aspirations of creating a positive difference in society and the lives of others. Living many life roles including wife, mother, sister, entrepreneur, businesswoman, and friend, she understands how life can be overwhelming sometimes and strives to help individuals of all ages keep a positive outlook and always put their best foot forward. Through her words and personal life stories, she motivates crowds, small and large, to live up to their potential, be the best version of themselves, and go after their dreams. Her motto of "Be Kind. Be Generous. Be Loving." promotes bringing three prominent life mannerisms back to the forefront of society and lifestyles in hopes that the world may be a little bit brighter. Ask her why she motivates people and her response is simple, "I'm just a good woman trying to be a better woman while inspiring the next man or woman. I just want to see everyone win, so I help where I can with what I can."

www.ingramcontent.com/pod-product-compliance
Lightning Source LLC
Chambersburg PA
CBHW071359290426
44108CB00014B/1607